THE LOOK BACK

~Landscapes and Elegies~

New and Selected Poems

Michael Jennings

THE LOOK BACK

Cover Image: *Stone Wash* by Mark Raush
Author Photo: Darryl Hughto
Book Design: Rowan Kehn

ISBN: 979-8-9868994-5-9

Turning Plow Press

For Suzanne and Shane

Author's Note

I began writing poems, I think, to summon up the Iranian landscape of my childhood and early youth, resulting over the years in something of a chronicle of one soul's interaction with the spirits of place: ritual soundings, in the ancient oral tradition, for the bones and colors of experience. I've always enjoyed small books of poems that could be experienced in one or two sittings, and I hope this book will be read simply as a collection of such small journeys within the arc of the larger plot. The landscapes and dreamscapes of my life—insofar as I've been able to conjure them, sculpt them, trick them into place—are, to me, sacred places that seem now to have always been there but needed the nudge and whisper of the Muse, who got where I needed to go, breathed life into the spirits I needed to dance with, and masqueraded as my remarkable wife for over 40 years, acting as both editor and auditor through all the stages of what Donald Hall called Goatfoot, Milktongue, and Twinbird, those most elemental aspects of the ancient art of poem-making.

Pardon me, if when I want
to tell the story of my life
it's the land I talk about.

Pablo Neruda *Still Another Day,* VI, trans. William O'Daly

CONTENTS

Book I:

DUST AND A GOOD WIND
(after the photographs of Dorothea Lange)

*A lion does not write a book, nor does the weather
erect a monument where the pride of a woman was
broken for want of a pair of shoes, or where a man
worked five years in vain to build a home and gave it up, bankrupt
and whipped...or where the wife went insane from sheer monotony
and blasted hope.*

J. Russell Smith, *North America.* 1925
—As recorded in Dorothea Lange's notes.

Six Tenant Farmers, Without Farms, Hardman County, Texas. 1938

Dust
and a good wind
will move mountains.

But these are not mountains,
only men. Each stands
with his own hat in his own pose,

and each stares into the blind eye of the camera
with almost the indifference
with which the blind sun stares. Their lives

have come to this. What moves on the horizon
no longer moves them. Like the dust storm's
gray aftermath, they are a stunned stillness

where the wind has been.
                          A dust storm begins
with a single gray particle, dislodged into wind
and looking for home. All heat and hunger,

it owns nothing and so has nothing to give.

What stands in the wind it demolishes.

What it has picked clean it leaves for the living.

Woman of the High Plains, Texas Panhandle. 1938

She stands, her long bones dark against the sky,
one hand on neck, the other pressed to her brow,
and she is laughing, as though out of nowhere
something had just dawned, as though somehow
something besides wind had passed through here
on its way to the mountains.
                    Listen:
out here the strained hollow faces of summer
grow stranger in winter, the moth-clouds get eaten
by bats from the north, and the long faces of worry
become the low eyeless dwellings of the horizon,
some small smoke rising from the chimneys.
                        Listen:
no one alive shall ever hear this laugh, or see
a woman in a flour sack with the posture of a heron
laugh like a child.
                Behind her the bleak plain
lies echoless, where even the birdcall of her bones
shall die
            under the bright clear rain of the million stars.

Damaged Child, Shacktown, Elm Grove, Oklahoma. 1936

The left eye
is an empty socket. A black stare
into blackness. Behind it: the gray brain that dreams
die back to, like a road map
found on the back seat
of an abandoned car. Shacktown, Elm Grove,
Oklahoma, a place
no one visits, a town that lives
on the rumor of rain.

The smile
is the Mona Lisa's, a vagueness
untouched by vagueness: if one can imagine that
of a half-wit child of eight
who stands in front of four pieces
of dark sheet-metal
that make up the side of a house a child
might throw rocks against
to make thunder.

I once planned
a trip to Nova Scotia, where distance
is decorative. Lakes, rivers: a gentle apportionment
of parts. Four months
went into the planning. It ended
by the side of a road
in a ditch, where a dead dog
grinned and glistened
in the rain.

I carry
a child somewhere in the dark
of my brain. A dead child. She reminds me
of the future. I give her names.
The names change. Today she stands
in front of four pieces of dark sheet-metal

and almost smiles. It is her birthday.
She has just turned eight.
Her one rag

is held together at her right shoulder
by a small knot that is almost a bow.

Child and Her Mother, Wapato, Yakima Valley, Washington. 1939

Her hair is long wet strands of dull black weed.
Her head, heavy with it, is bowed. Her eyes
look toward, but do not see, the ground that lies
like iron at her feet. Her fingers knead
and push the barbed wire fence her body's greed
would fold around. But though the one barb tries
to pierce the flesh, the floral dress despise
its thread, the small belly will not take seed.

Her mother stands behind, hand on hip. She'd
rather she stood elsewhere and not be wise
and know down to her bones that no surprise
will come today, that they will not be freed.
Yet she stands, shades her eyes, mouthing a creed
gone bad, wishing it might be otherwise
than to get up each day to the same skies,
hoping there might be something left to bleed.

But sun has honed their land to bone, and grain
no longer tries to flower. The sky is lead,
the days are long, and nothing in a dream
can change the way their shadows seem to stain
the ground, or make them go, or how the dead
come drifting like the echo of a stream

where no stream flows.
                              So let the body steam
in the long night. Let all the shapes of dread
come welling up in the tired shards of brain
until the eyes of child and mother teem
with murder. No help comes to the dark head.
No black blood's pounding brings the vengeance of rain.

On the Great Plains, Near Winner, South Dakota. 1938

On the Great Plains, near Winner, South Dakota,
winters are long. Philosophy is short.
What goes under snow in November
emerges again in March, sometimes later,
sometimes changed. Life's hard. Daughters
get names like Hope or Faith. Sons
don't get far, or move away
altogether, their letters coming back
full of the emptiness they left with.

And here in the space of what looks like
half a mile, maybe less, three churches stand,
one behind the other, like reflections
of the same church: each painted white,
each with its single black spire
thrust into the northern sky. Nothing else
stands or grows, but the prairie grass
moving away like a whisper.

But distance can be tricky here,
so that the church that stands near the horizon
may be a day's walk, maybe farther. And in deep snow
the situation worsens. Destinations are measured
in yards or feet, sometimes inches. Direction,
too, can be confusing. A man goes
snow-blind quickly in a blizzard, sound
distorts, the mind grows muddled.
                              It is said in the desert
a man never dies of thirst
but he will first see water. Here it is said,
a man never freezes to death
but he can hear the ringing of bells.

Grayson, San Joaquin Valley, California. 1938

Say, for a moment, there is this building, too broad
or close for the picture, which looms in the picture
like a bad dream, an image pressed
half on the mind's eye, half onto some darkness
just out of reach.
              Lines of raw clapboard cross
from frame to frame, while the rooftree, centered,
lets in two triangles of sky: gray, as the building
is gray, but paler, flatter, if anything
more coincidental than the crude structure
that hulks like a bad conscience on a bleak plain
we do not see, but feel, a dull ache of distance
that comes these last miles to lie in the open crawlspace
like a dark stain.
              And the building hangs like that,
in air, between earth and sky, darkness and sun,
and rivets the eye like a pale scar.
              Or say it is a building
built to be come to, built like the men who built it,
who, if they knew little of heaven, knew what they needed
of wood and iron, that is made wholly
of wood and iron, built like a hobnail boot.
              And say
dead center in the picture, a man lies, that the building
surrounds him as though he had dreamed it, as though
he had nailed each board. But say he is only
a gunny sack with ankles, a corpse left in the shade
where the rotting is slower.
              Whether church,
or school, or meeting hall, say it is a building
where men came to listen, its floor and benches
full of splinters, the wind through its boards
a groaning of iron.
              Or say the possibilities
run out, that it is a building built by men who spoke prose
and died without fanfare.
              Say there is this silence.

Walking Wounded, Oakland. 1954

There is a moment, albeit hypothetical,
when something foreign
                passing through something familiar
leaves only a blackness,
                a record of travel.

                                Blood bulges
                and overruns the hole,
and sometimes a scream flaps out
                from the first O
                                of astonishment,
the face gathering darkness like a hole
                that will never again
                                get quite filled in.

The man in this corridor
                is pure darkness,
                                the forest floor,
a black loam you could lie down in
                dreaming of the long rays of sunlight
                                that never come.
                It is dream from which no one wakes.

The man in this corridor
                intrudes
                                almost
not at all: a black shoulder, a black pant leg,
                a dead foot and thin line of black crutch
                                angling
from behind a telephone pole.
                                There's no body,
                only darkness reshuffling.
No face, only a meeting of moles
                holding silent parley
                                in an unmarked grave.

A city is closing
             on the man in this photograph. The telephone pole
looks broad as a door, and the blank wall
             that is the whole right side of the picture
                          looms, somehow,
closer.
             It is washed whiter than any scar.

Toquerville, Utah 1953

Whatever it was, it happened here, sometime after rain
in Toquerville. You walked toward a wall, the progress
slow. It leaned toward you, cracking, as if
trying to accommodate to vague shifts of sunlight
or weather. The scorched air crackled
like an old newsreel (in it men drop like flies, rise
up again, salute and fall back). There was the sound
of rain, a little wind; and slowly the wall took on
a blotchy, blood-splattered look: an enemy wall,
greasy with old deceits, muffled cries.

                                       Then the late sun,
sliding into a windowpane, reflected a small path
through the forest, though there was no forest,
only the deceptions of sun in late summer
when the roads, even after rain, stay dusty,
haggard, as from men marching.

                                 You arrived,
flagging, unhealthy. You felt somehow
more like your grandfather: weak-eyed, troubled,
a face forever slashed by a pale blur of sunlight
you are always approaching.

                             Even into twilight.

                                    Turn now
and face this camera full face, the wall
behind you. Remember the evidence,
your grandfather's face: starched, formal.
Remember the patched plaster of faces,
it is all you will ever have to remember.
Remember when the pieces come together
in the cold porcelain of your mind's eye,
it will be someone else's grandfather
who stares out, bland and unblemished,
wearing your face. You will be gone then.
It will be sometime after rain in Toquerville.

Man Stepping From Curb. 1956

This blind black stepping
into gray this gathering
of light around dark
edges this hanging headless
weightless this hungering
for loose hair and wide
thighs this too taut
skin in too slack
air this hope despair this
running through fingers stone
in the hand empty waking hanged
man thief this gathering
of night dispersing
of stars this flapping
in the breeze this anger
this loneliness this wide
emptiness falling into
stars ether this rise
again into ossified
earth this walking waking
dark angel hanging…

Moon forever rising.
Sun forever falling.
Reflect.   Reflect.

Book II:

SUMMONING THE OUTLAWS

*The Americans are certainly hero worshippers, and always take
their heroes from the criminal classes.*

—Oscar Wilde, in St. Louis, on hearing of the death of Jesse James

Horse Scapes

Remington's bronze broncs are curs,
each renegade muscle
the bulge of a new start
demanding blood. His rider
is Poseidon taming the waves,
his hat a flagrant tool
and insignia,
wind-creased and nautical.

The Indian ponies are more soulful,
painted into the plains like desert flowers
or whirling dust storms.

Under it all, behind it all—
mesa, arroyo, castle rock or butte—
in splendor or bereavement,
the ancient dirt.

Bad Men of the Old West

They are mostly skinny men with big eyes and scuzzy beards
who died ragged in holey socks
with so many bullet holes in their bodies
you can hardly count them,
and yet their memento mori photographs,
in which they are propped up by the grim townsfolk
or laid out in a buckboard or on an undertaker's slab,
startle us with the banality of their quietude
after so much violence.
We have killed here the devil's spawn
the photographs seem to say,
here are the wages of sin,
and we are neither proud nor sorry.
They passed through like any spell of bad weather
and we went back to our commonplace lives
in our kitchens and on our front porches,
and wrote ballads and dime novels about them
as if they were anything but poor angry men gone astray,
imagining them all steely-nerved and remorseless,
pretending we never killed them.

Black Elk

once rode into battle with only a ceremonial bow
thrust out before him so he became an arrowing
Thunder God, and the Bluecoats ran.
Crazy Horse was scarier still, a phantom fire, unkillable.
But the mountains failed them, and the grasses
failed them, and the rivers.
So much Spirit eradicated in 50 years.
So much Sorrow.
So little space to be alone with the alone.
So little time to walk in the sun.

Jesse James

His was my first death, laid out on a slab
on the red framed cover of the *Frontier Times*
when I was eight: his "doctor's beard"
and up-curved closed eyelids like angel wings:
benevolent, almost saintly. I learned later,
of course, through a slew of biographies,
that he was a truly bad man, angry,
vengeful, planning to slit the throat
of the bank teller in his next derring-do;
but straight-backed and aristocratic,
handsome, with a sense of humor,
loyal in his own way, but every bit
a child of war, christened in the blood
of the land.
        Haunted years by this picture
and the odd ambivalence surrounding
this King of Outlaws, I've learned
what about death? —how slyly it grins
when you're just trying to square up the frame?

The Long Riders

Lawmen who entered Robbers' Roost country
came on white horses, wanting to be seen
from a long way off, sending a sign
they were just passing through. No fools,
they knew the hard-leather long riders
manning their secret passes, mountain strongholds,
who crossed long miles of pitiless Red Desert
past Dry Gulch and the Dirty Devil River,
through Lost Soldiers Pass, Cataract Canyon,
past Salt Wash, Poison Springs, Castle Gate, Big Hole,
across Sam's Mesa, Diamond Mountain,
through Dry Fork, Buckhorn Wash, Stump Creek Pass,
Star Valley, Alder Gulch, Uintah Basin,
along Vermillion Creek and the Pariah River,
thinning the cattle barons' herds, emptying
their banks, waylaying their payroll trains,
and shooting up the towns they partied in.
They made their names the way poor men could
and so passed into legend. For a short span,
they were the gods of God's hard country,
who died mostly as they wished, drunk or sober,
with their boots on.

The Fury of Geronimo

His name, associated forever
with relentless destruction, is thought
to have come from his knife attack
on a line of Mexican riflemen
praying haplessly to St. Jerome
once he'd closed ground
on them.
             They'd taken
everything he loved—
wife, mother, children,
mowed down like grass
in the grass—

and no matter your aim,
you can't kill a ghost.

Hickok

with pistols the best shot
anyone in the West ever saw,
going blind in New York,
got word young guns
in two towns he'd marshalled
claimed he'd never dare show again,
and so sent for posting
in their newspaper windows
the baddest frontier poem ever written
"I arrive in your prairie dog towns on Tuesday.
I wear my hair long as usual."

Apart from Wild Bill, only brass bands showed up.

Myth

1.

I visited The Kid's grave around 1960—
neglected, weed-choked, tawdry,
the gravestone squint,
surrounded by a little iron fence
a child could step over.
The nothingness I walked away with
stretched out blue
into big New Mexican sky.

He got to be the dime novel hero he dreamed of,
though we know only a little of what he did,
desperate in a desperate land, lightning
in the night sky, a singer and a dancer,
stealing fire and taking the consequences,

this kid we came to lament.

2.

¿Quién es?

In handwriting immaculate
as any gentleman's of his day,
though considerably less fenced in by commas,
he wrote to the governor who would betray him,
I am not afraid to die like a man fighting
but I would not like to be killed like a dog unarmed.

In the end the law was just the other gang,
backed by the bankers, who sent their assassins
to murder him in the dark in his stocking feet.
Death came anonymously as it had
to Siegfried, skewered in the back
in the name of justice.

Comanche Moon

meant death on the Texas plains, that bone-white light
where the horned, black-faced, stone-age
demons of vengeance rode like shadows
of death over the mesas, along trails
few men could trace even in daylight.
They were crueler than the prairies
or the Texas Blue Northers,
crueler than death.
They'd roast you on a spit and laugh,
scoop out your brains while you were still breathing.
They lived so close to the prairie
they were the prairie; it mapped their hearts.
They were magicians with horses,
better light cavalry than Genghis Khan's
Mongols, or the Parthians—
able to tame a mustang in minutes
or steal a horse while his rider slept, one rein
tied to his wrist.
                    But in the noonday sun
the bleached bones of their buffalo
stretched farther than the eye could see,
their ponies murdered by the thousands.
They learned no pitiless savage sun god
could ever match the intricacies
of Christian hypocrisy
or the murderous Comanche
that grew in every Texan heart.

Speak Spirit

sing the far-sighted anger of Red Cloud,
baddest Bad Face in the Black Hills and Badlands,
who killed as easily as Achilles,
had the strategic cunning of Odysseus,
and gathered the war tribes like god-like Agamemnon.
Speak of the bridling of his fiery wrath,
his stone-faced rise from low tribe-status
to become Chief among Chiefs, moving like a panther
to beat down the Cheyenne, Shoshone, Pawnee,
Kiowa, Ute, and the straight-toothed, most hated Crow,
doubling the coup counted by Sitting Bull,
outfoxing Sherman and the U.S. Army,
sending the beautiful and almost girlish
wavy haired Crazy Horse to moon the Bluecoats
to give chase, their repeating rifles
hushed by the hissing of a thousand arrows.
Mention his passing into life as statesman
in white men's clothes in a White Man house,
meeting with Grant and Congress, viewing
the U.S. Armory like writing on the wall,
who could say, almost without bitterness,
they made us many promises, more than
I can remember, but they kept only one.
They promised they would take our land and they did.
Whisper the stillness of Red Cloud,
a warrior worthy a Homeric hymn.

Ghost Dance, 1890

We wanted them to live in square boxes
while everything they loved was round
like the world. Most found
farming a farce. They got Jesus
but not the White People who brought him.
They decided to dance them away,
the square-footeds, dance so the Iron Horse
would die in its tracks, dance the return
of the limitless grasses and their hooved
brothers and sisters, dance the return
of rivers to their true names and earth
free again of hoarders and marauders.
And then they were slaughtered
in a circle of Bluecoats
for dancing.

Book III:

ALMA'S HOUSE

where you could see

Deeper into the country than you expected
And discovered that the field beyond the hedge
Grew more distinctly strange as you kept standing
Focused and drawn in by what barred the way.

—Seamus Heaney "Field of Vision"

Alma's House

I keep seeing this muddy, sometimes sunbaked road
from Alma's crooked porch on the Negro side
of Beaumont, Texas circa 1955.
It's where I stayed when my parents were away,
a world of tumble-down shacks and angry
young men that Alma kept at bay
whenever I was out there. Except for Nick,
Alma's husband who sometimes mowed our lawn,
I knew only the women, who took me to church
in their big white dresses and enormous hats
and sang hymns as if they meant them.
Nick called me *Honey* and stroked my hair.
He was the color of dried tobacco leaves
and seemed older and more tired
than any man I'd ever known, but also kinder.
Maybe he'd once been a great hell-raiser,
a razor in his pocket and a bottle in a bag
like men I later met on trains, trading swigs
and stories and a sense of fate
hurtling at us out of the night sky.
But there was no Devil in Nick in my day,
only a kind of fatherly Job.
They fed me mustard greens and collard greens
and okra, dark aromas that made their house
exotic with its tilting floors and peeling linoleum,
and let me sleep in their bed and play
with Alma's nearly blind little black retriever
and Nick's skinny flea-bitten hound, chained
to his house out back. They taught me
to stay out of the way of the gargantuan geese,
the real watch dogs, and to feed the chickens,
and visit Ida, the coffee-colored hairdresser
next door, who'd do all the neighborhood
ladies in her big, hardwood living room
while everybody laughed and Alma smoked
cigarettes, which I'd never seen before.
But I never went down that rutted dirt road

beyond Alma's house that seemed to go nowhere
but into weeds and more collapsing shacks
and maybe some swampland nobody wanted.
When she died I was a freshman in college
and Nick wrote asking for money.
I sent him $10, half my week's allowance.
Sorry, I wrote. Sorry.

Dancing at the Silver Dollar

By day it was a big dreary barn of a place,
but at night it was lit up like stars on the prairie,
the only hot spot in Bandera, a town fed
by dude ranches and tourist trade
with old west storefronts and wooden sidewalks
just like the movies, stores that sold boots
and Stetsons and moccasins, all the attire
of weekend cowboys and cowgirls
who flocked on Saturday nights to the dance hall
called the Silver Dollar, where the steel guitar
sent shivers up your spine like a breeze in the live oaks,
and the women twirled and the men sashayed,
and the sheriff moseyed in with a .38 riding
like a small boat on the fleshy sea of his right hip
as I worked up the nerve to ask the girl to dance
with an outbreak of psoriasis on her right hand
my father said I shouldn't mention and didn't.
She was seven and I was eight—the full extent
of our conversation as we circled the room
doing the two-step, cute as proverbial buttons,
with the whisper of moccasins and the stomping of boots
not quite heaven but close as I'd ever come
to the leathery heart of Texas.

Skateland

was where the beautiful hoods came
with their beautiful-thighed girlfriends
in their dainty skating skirts
and ice-cream smiles.
The chromeless gleam of their late 40s hotrods
blazing in the parking lot,
the iron-polished crease of their Levi's
more carefully wrought
than any tuxedo pant, they darted
through the crowd with knees bent and hips
swaying to the Wurlitzer burble,
nonchalant as bayou kings and princes
in Lafitte's Barataria tradition—
Dicky Thibodaux with his one glass eye
that made him all the dreamier,
Eugene in his shiny ducktail.
They had a saint-like purity of being
that was steely and lethal.
I longed to be like them, immaculate
and mythical
                    under the swirling lights.

Remembering the Alamo

It seemed half the schools in the state
were named Bowie or Crockett
and most of the other half either
Stephen F. Austin or Sam Houston.
They were the patron saints of the only religion
that mattered and necessitated a yearly
pilgrimage to the Mecca of the Alamo,
there to ponder the great sword of a knife
that had made history on some remote sandbar
or other, and the tiny room its namesake
met his end in, there in his tubercular
death bed to be shot through the head
more times than anyone really wanted to count,
and contemplate Crockett's portrait,
his almost girlish face and long Tennessee hair
that would have gotten him laughed out
of any 1950's bar in Texas, if not killed.
Of course, we never imagined the true savagery
of the event, or the suspect motives of the gang of thieves
who wanted to steal a whole country pretty much
in the name of Whiteness. We were true believers.
We wanted to step across a line in the sand,
face down thousands, hear our names shouted
like oaths over the blazing green battlefields of our past.

Uncle V.J.

Uncle V.J. lived in a roomy shack
a bit off the highway near Vidor,
a more than usually rough neck of the woods in East Texas,
where he kept a passel of hound dogs and fed us the first
and best venison stew I ever had. He wore mustard shirts
(were they also floral?) wide open to the waist
so that the full forest of chest and stomach hair
sort of poured out, this above baggy brown pants
and bedroom slippers he shuffled around in. After dinner,
he'd haul me onto his lap, laughing, mussing my hair,
and promise me a hound pup from his next litter
while my mother squirmed in her chair
and my father cracked out some bourbon to talk business.

Years later I asked him just who *was* Uncle V.J.
Not your uncle, he said. What he was was a timber thief,
and your Uncle Rex and I owned some land up that way
and would try to sell him the timber off it before he could steal it.
He might have been a very rich man, but he'd get drunk
every couple of years and kill someone with his knife
in a bar fight, and then he'd have to pay Percy Foreman
(700 acquittals out of 701 murder cases)
  to get him off, and that cost him half what he owned.

Well, I guess half of what you own every couple of years
and you end up in a shack with a passel of hound dogs,
which, so far as I could tell, was just how Uncle V.J. liked it.
They finally did send him up for two years in Huntsville
for stabbing, but not quite killing, his brother-in-law.

Leon

My stepfather was not much of a talker
and even less a storyteller. He did once
confide that in his youth a mare or cow
was deemed 'stunt-broke' if you could climb on a stool
and fuck her without getting kicked.
I kind of blanched at that, preferring
to hear how he once watched Pretty Boy Floyd
rob the town bank while loading hundred pound
sacks of potatoes at the country store,
or how his old horse, Tex, plodding his paper route,
would let him sleep the whole way home, till Tex
landed them both in a dry ditch, himself
having sleep-walked off the small wooden bridge.

But I could never really make him out
more than a glimpse back at the old homestead
in a town burdened by the sick-sweet reek of paper mills,
the noxious rot-stink of the black soil itself,
visiting an old couple from his childhood,
moonshine served ceremoniously in quart jars,
to hear stories of family migrations
that began, "back in aught six" or "in 19
and 25," stories I couldn't much follow
or at least didn't. Lightless, musty kitchen,
ancient farm table, he a gaunt white ghost
mumbling somewhere off in a corner, she
a pair of ropy blue arms dangling from
a grimy gray sack dress. They called him Lee-on,
happy to see the boy next door grown up,
become a world traveler. I was too young
and privileged to truly see *them*,
or understand how firmly planted
their cheese-colored feet were
in their own piece of earth, however poisonous.

Book IV:

CONFESSION OF SAND,
CELEBRATION OF WIND

For my brother, Stephen

For beauty's nothing
but the beginning of Terror we are still just able to bear, and why
we adore it so is because it serenely distains to destroy us.

—Rilke *Duino Elegies*, translated by Stephen Spender

Ur of the Chaldees, 1958

They are like aliens on the moon, the Americans—
bermuda shorts and cameras, pudgy, pale,
a little queasy from the train ride.
Dust from the storm in the night
has permeated everything they own
down to the skin.
They are not quite certain why they came,
and wear the baffled, blinking looks of baby birds.

The hole in the ground is the biggest I've ever seen,
with "evidence of the flood" — a four-foot-wide ribbon
of sand half way up the sides of an otherwise brown pit
strewn with broken bits of pottery. Local kids, urchins,
scamper down the steep, thin path at break-neck speed
for *rials* and *dinars*. They seem to have sprung up here
without benefit of parents or care. Across
the millennia, I feel the closeness of children
and the terrible price of money.

After a long climb, I am first to reach the summit
of the ziggurat
and so enter the dusky sky of Abraham.
I am 10. My heart is a drum.
I stand at the top of the god-forsaken world.

Hanoon

Our cook, Hanoon, tells me he is a Chaldean,
displaced by who knows how many migrations,
murders, to come to live in Braim Village
along the river green with date palms,
cool in its dark mud huts even in summer,
though he must ride to our house across
the blazing salt flats on a comic huge bicycle
wearing a pith helmet. His teeth are oddly dark
along the gums, though serving as wire cutters
when he needs them.
                              He wrings the neck of a chicken
and we laugh to see it scuttle in crazed circles
crashing into the walls of the compound. So death
is right here with us always, and maybe
we too are crazy chickens.
                              When I am eleven,
we come to dine at his village. He is something
like a Head Man, and we are given *fesenjahn*
that looks like mud and tastes like ambrosia.
We eat from a common bowl with our hands,
and for the first time I feel holy.
                              In the bazaar,
the beggar boys scatter like startled birds
at a single hissing whisper from his lips,
his hands fluttering like quick black bats.
                              For hours
he squats at cards, slapping them down with true
gambler's relish — his big, bare, broad feet,
so quiet as he pads, cat-like, about the house,
planted happily on the wide earth,
his pock-marked face smiling
like a black leopard's.
                              Years later,
we'll lure him with money to another town
far from his family and tribe,
to live, displaced, among the grim Bakhtiari.
And he will service us, less smiling than before,

and steal our silver, and we will fire him,
and I will know what it is like
to steal a man's joy and pride
and break his heart.

In my dreams, I break bread with him still.

View of a Wedding: The Fat Man

We've come on horseback deep into the hills
for this, along sand roads hardened by crude oil
and blazing sun.
                  I am sitting next to the Fat Man,
intrigued by the watermelon biceps bulging his suit coat
as he crushes beer cans between two fat fingers
at least a decade before the aluminum can's
invention.
            When he finishes one, I hand him another
"Careful," whispers Khosrow, "when he gets drunk
he kills people."
            The bride is a child about 13
and skinny as a boy. She goes through the ceremony
with the wide-eyed, dutiful look of a kindergarten kid
in a school play.
            The groom, too, looks terrified.
After the vows, they retire to a room to consummate
the marriage while the women trill like cicadas
and the men do the sword dance with crude sticks—
ancient, elaborate, no doubt dangerous.
                  Kahbelli, my groom,
who tends my horse like a wet-nurse to the crown prince,
and whose village this is, wears the same baggy, brown uniform
he does day-in, day-out.
            When I ask to take his photograph,
he braces to attention like a palace guard—
stooped, skinny shoulders pulled back, the haggard,
kind face, always with a day's growth of beard,
stern and almost proud.
            When Khosrow proffers
a full 8-ounce tumbler of vodka, he downs it
with a single draft, bows and offers a slight salute
and begins a little baggy-panted dance, Appalachian
almost, or Ozark.
            The music is drum and whiney, reedy horn
that brings the hills down close, that is ghost dance
and night pulse, that lulls the Fat Man to sleep

and brings out the groom with his bloody handkerchief
to a cry that splits the night,
                              vaulting the two drunken
Englishmen into the sword dance ring
for their predictable corn-hole parody
that makes the villagers laugh
                              and the Fat Man snore
and night close over us in a blaring of horns.

Horse

Here is the relic of Bronze Age glory no teenage boy
can quite shake from his daydream — the lust of Achilles,
the soft curve of haunch that tempts theft
under the cover of moonlight beyond neighboring hills.
Alexander's eyes rolled and flashed like horses' eyes.
The Great Khan's Standard was a horse's skull.

But this is mere tribal mare, circa 1960, gaunt
as Picasso's horse under a rider thin as shadow.
But spirit still channels through the twin poles of the neck.
Mood plays out in the whim of leaf-shaped ears.
She knows she was made for travel and moves
with the accustomed grace of a dancer

over white flats in liquid blue heat, over red rock
aglow each night from the fires of a hundred oil flares,
on some errand ancient as Ur, tied to death or birth—
whose rider would rather starve than sell her—
whose solemn cheek is a barge prow in the moonlight,
patient on the breathing river—
                              who mothered the thunder.

A Man Squatting in the Shade

As if one with the plowed contours of carved rock
where the sunlight has taken centuries
to cultivate its dead, he squats and stares
at the land's long shudder to the horizon.

Only the one slow hand, fumbling from time
to time among the stones, and the loud bark
of rock on rock throbbing into the cliffs
disturb the bright perfection of this day—

the dark face flinching with the contact. What
but the first quick act of murder, half-conceived,
the smooth downward arc of the first chipped rock
splintering the mind, could hold him here,
                                    where he
survives in a six-foot circle of life—
in the scorpion's country, but in Cain's land.

Heat

Day without plot. Fixtured and fissured. Fractured beyond
measure.

I have known heat to stretch horizon to horizon
like bright steel — a metal or mica or star-scattered heaven
foundering the mind. Thick-tongued and wordless. White sand
on black brain. Blood rivered in suet. A pocket
picked empty as wind.
Nothing moves in such heat,
not lizard or scorpion, sand-fly or shadow. Tree
becomes rock, becomes gray husk, becomes
ruinous. Squalor of sand. Numbness of sun.
To squat there,
the stones of your absence in your hands,
is to squat in the center of silence forever.
It is to hold the sun like water in the crumbling of your hands.

****

It is to hold the bright day. Sun. Sand. A dun-colored dog

disappearing into a distance of sun and sand—
humped, slavering. The steady
rise and fall of the four flickering paws
too maniacally silent and concentrated for even
the loose gesture of wind to intrude on.
                                    Or the dream of day,
a child's sorrowing and dreaming — aftermath
of that too much excitement. Four boys with baseball bats
who had braved what they knew of the horrors
of the desert, a compound of mad dogs
and oil drums,
                barbed-wire and heat,
a dun-colored dog disappearing into desert like a dead wind.

****

It hangs like a daydream of fish in the sun's eye. Fish flying

like birds above the thunder of dynamite, burble of river,
then falling to flotsam. Fish by the armload,
blind, dazed, flaccid as faith. A stench
ripping open the whole length of the gullet of sky
luring foxes and flies.
                              A day I walked in sun
unstable as the dynamite I carried in a brown paper sack
like in indigestible lunch.
                              And threw. And walked. And threw.
And watched the shards of hillside rise
like torn brains to hang in the hair of scrub-trees
while the lizard sang silent in the sun — the blood-
throated lizard, bloated and bragging in the swaggering sun.

****

Or the daydream of glass. White light. Bone light. The sailing of
glass—

Shards of pottery heaped in domes
where ziggurats grew round in wind
and the tombs of kings
stunk with centuries of fox.
The sun was a blind mad eye
carved on an obsidian stairway to heaven
where the fallen bulls of stone
offered their great backs to me to ride
and dust filled the air like glass.
Mother's eyes were black fires
as she hurled ashtrays and plates, bowls and crystal
at walls and mirrors. Her voice
was glass breaking. Her breath was ether.
The stench of fox,
like the burning of flesh, stayed in my nostrils for days.

****

A dream before I knew you, met you. Though I knew of your
                                                    absence.

I knew of Lydia Cathcart who spread her great thighs
on the Riding Club couch or across
the great outcropped boulders of the desert
for grooms and stable hands.
                            I knew of her husband's
straw-colored pomaded hair and creased
high-fashion trousers,
                        and how her eyes bugged out a little
and spittle formed at the edges of her mouth.
                                        Akbar,
who would die in the advanced stages of syphilis,
served our drinks and food, laughed
like a girl, and kissed me when he could.
I knew of your absence. And I dreamed of Lydia Cathcart.

                        ****

And of women on horseback — long shadows in the deep hills.

And one who rode a stallion like a black wind
that even I could not ride,
      her hair a raven black.
And then the horse who fell and bled for me,
a deep pocket of blood forming between his forelegs
like a breast—
     a black horse with a girl's mane
and a king's name.
      And then the dream of women
ridden by men or boys
in the twilit paddock, moving
down the long hill in the long heat, arm
in arm, indifferent to all but the long loneliness
of the first stars rising,
     the glittering of raw, fierce weapons.

      ****

And the desert rises then in the twilight. It lifts

its burnt body out of itself. The scabs of its flesh
soften. It sings in its silence like an old woman
and becomes young again.
                              Her sands glitter in moonlight.
Her ridges rise like deep rivers entering the sea of stars.
Her foxes find new stealth,
                        their fur bristles.
Snakes slither from dark dens with eyes like stars
and tongues like the singing of stars.
                              This is the clarity
of fire.
       This is the clarity of the long bones of the hills
rubbing together like the thighs of the long women
buried among them.
                 This is death.
This is the white-hot crotch of death, blue as a diamond.

****

And Gafoor smokes his hookah with yellow eyes. Rocks

and claps his thighs. Dreams himself. Stinks of horse,
stinks of women, stinks of the sun and the sun's lies,
the long ride.
        And the round stones of the moonlight
are the hunched backs of the night's feeders
who rise and walk—
        Or the arched bellies of the night's
eaten. Who do not get up. Who turn on themselves
like sculpture. Blue stones.
        And the tarantula
rising like smoke
        sings to his green-eyed mate
under the arched light of her dark sting,
and dances there in the round light.
        Long night.
The yellow-eyed. Soft-thighed. Torn and turning.

****

And then shard-light in the broken east and the stones' cry—

the huddled bones,
carcass and carcass. Confession of sand,
celebration of wind.
           And bright blood blooms in the desert
as the blind white fish
flounder from withered pond
to withered pond
where once the river flowed hard
in the moonlight.
           Achilles died
that Odysseus might live — the heartless heart
succumbing to the body's stealth,
              the moon-fired fox,
skulking and singing, meeting the dawn's dead eye.

****

O daughter of days. Mother of nights. If I have sought women

as the sun
seeks water,
          eye
in eye,
      tear
         and muscle,
                forgive me the long chains'
shackle and shackle. Forgive me the great bull-bones
of the world in the sun,
               and hold me now in the implacable
pallor of your gaze, this improbable poise
of full moon at dawn's edge—
                 Bone-song,
                     wind-haunt,
voice of the fathers
and the father of voice—
            Bring back
the great wind,
        sing me the singing,
               the great song—

O blood of the mothers who labored long!

Inner Sanctum

Anood and Matrood Jassemzahdi
have long since moved from their home by the courts
to the low mud huts of Braim Village.
Years have passed since our tennis days
and I am crossing the barren flats for the last time,
feeling the heat rise through the soles of my shoes,
seeing it waver, silvery-blue, as the black-green
date palms near the river grow
imperceptibly closer.
                              The heat is an odd familiar.
It holds me in its palm like a puppet.
The dizzying distance of the flats to the north
could be glare ice, polar smoke, or the timeless lake
it once was.
                    Miles and miles and miles
the mind sails as the feet plod
a few hundred yards. Sunstroke, heatstroke,
are states of mind almost religious, the body
spooling off into darkness.
                              The narrow
dark paths of the village are welcoming
labyrinthine passageways, silvery-blue
eyes of trachoma flickering in the shadows.
My hands grope for a few cool coins
to assuage the heat of conscience.
                              The doorway
is there — a few low-ceilinged rooms
fanning off from the courtyard, palatial
by village standards — the swept dirt floors,
open spigot in the courtyard,
and the *chador*-draped figures of Mother
and Sister, two silent hearth goddesses
of the cave-cool gloom, mourners of a life
more ancient than I can imagine.
                              In just such a room
Christ, the wanderer, must have had his weary feet bathed,
with just such sure strong hands as theirs.

                              And for his crown
he must have worn just such camelthorns
as I have idly scuffed in coming—
                         anything like a rose

rare in these parts.

Old Mountains

There were mountains in the old place,
the place of old bones, and the mountains
were like bones, only browner, sandstone,
though sometimes bleached pale as bones.
And dark goats moved among them,
and the people who grew out of them
were like goats, small and dark
and quick when the sun was not pure
poison, moving about their business
which was not our business, theirs
being soil, which there wasn't much of,
ours being oil, which came out of the ground
by the ton and snaked through the hills
and desert in pipelines inevitable
as the azure, steel sky itself. Perhaps
they were not real mountains so much
as up-thrust foothills, craggy plateau
a man or goat could climb in a day,
stand at the top of, and feel Moses
come down from.
                    They were holy mountains,
and under the holy mountains was oil
that sometimes still made bushes burn
or the Red Sea part for the islands
of deep-bellied freighters, pregnant
with crude.
                    And if they were not mountains,
they were at least the high steppes
of the horsemen, grown ghostly with time,
and my sleeper's body slept among them,
and my dreamer's body, which was only smoke
from village chimneys in winter, or the black
eyes of the skulls of their huts in summer,
saw the quick shimmering emerald of the fields
and crevices in spring, the flash of the bright-dressed
girls of the waterhole, their ankle bracelets
saucy as the glitter of crime in Salome's eyes,

and the black eyes under the black wind
of the black *chadora*
billowing around the husks of crones.
They were the sacred mountains camped
at our outskirts, while our fathers
mined oil from beneath them and hardly
saw them.
         But their graves sang to us
in the evenings, and the thin smoke
of their cook-fires rose like ghosts,
and they lay down with us in our dreams
like beasts, breathing and patient.
                        "Ours,"
we thought, as the Persian blue sky
swaddled their shoulders, as the black
night sky lay down on their backs
with its pinprick stars. They rose
like continents in the black sea
of nightfall, then rose again like the skulls
of sacrificial beasts in the dawn. And perhaps
our white mothers heard them and started
drinking harder, savaging the servants,
quarreling with our sad sack fathers.
Distracted in the midnight, they paced cold tiles,
their bare feet lisping the hours—
ethereal, haughty, silken whisperings.
And the mountains were theirs, too,
and the dirty hands of the servants
who needed such scolding. Some absence
lurked in their eyes like the shadows
of mountains, among the coffee klatches
and beer-swilling mornings.
               But we
were the children of the mountains,
and they entered us as easily as sky,
as easily as night, and what they showed us
was fire and shadow, dancers under the worn moon.
And we saw how time moved in ripples toward the horizon,
shuddering under the noonday sun. They moved
in us like the spirits of Alexander or Herod,
Nebuchadnezzar, Ashurbanipal, Xerxes

or Artaxerxes — slow fires
in the waking midnight.
                        And our incongruous
fathers waited at the bus stop — white,
short-sleeved shirts, clip-on ties
and crew cuts. They talked of Oklahoma
or L.A., Atlantic City or Baton Rouge,
but never of the bleached mountains
on the hem of whose skirts they stood
dazed in the morning light. Their gaze
was too calculated, the sheaves of paper
in their briefcases too diagrammatic
and impersonal. Children of the Depression,
their souls had suffered foreclosure.
They had bankers' eyes.
                        They are mostly
dead now, copies of *Forbes Magazine*
strewn on the night table. And we
who were children of the mountains
search nightly on the News for glimpses
of the pale, pitiless sleepers — there
behind the reporter with blank banker's eyes,
beyond the rolling dust of tanks, bomb blasts
and squalor, the rubble of apocalypse.
We have joined the absent ones.
Nothing there now remembers us
but the mountains
                        etched behind our eyelids.

Book V:

WHERE SHE DANCES

During the dismal months the soul sat shrunken and lifeless,
but the body took the straight path to you.
The night bellowed.
By stealth we milked the cosmos and survived.

—Tomas Transtromer, "Firescribbbling"

The past was terrible. I sat beside myself
near the river of bones. The low hanging leaves
called to me, threatening my waters.
I pretended not to be listening. I killed
the river's fish, picked tree bark.
I said to myself, this is my hand, this is my eye,
and this the world I bring to my mouth.
But who is that tree moving like water,
who is that dark and smooth shining water
growing into your eyes, becoming the smell
of moss in the palms of your hands? And why
does it mirror my hand, my mouth, my eye?
So all day now, I paint you, sing you, see you.
I give you a home in the bones of the mountain.

Where She Dances

Purple jaguar midnight
of lost imaginings—ebony, jet,
obsidian lakes of fire—
hers are the drumbeat spanking of bare
hard feet, far off wafting of laughter.

Come dance with the daughter
of rag-tag summer. See the turn
of her fiery wrist. Moon
paints her shadow. Sun
cannot find her. The fierce stars

bring her to bliss.
Once she was tree trembling in moonlight.
Once she was river
tied down by her hair.
Once she was wind, once she was breath—

now only flame
in the flare
of a pupil,
a delicate rustle's
velvety purr.

When the River Flutters

her wings, she is no longer the Amazon
floating the crescent moon as her navel,

she is your shadow rising to meet you.
The nightsilk mountains bend close.

Something in the lisping silence grieves,
exalts, dies its thousand deaths.

Your body is also a river with wings,
with talons, a place of betrayals

where shadowy gods, horned
or with twisting serpents for hair

are drowned, torn to shreds,
then rise again into stars.

Tomorrow, at dawn,
something shaggy will come down,

peering out from the night-drugged leaves,
dazzled by the spokes of new sun.

Her Dalliance

Between her fingers
the plucked stalk of your brainstem
blossoms

petal by petal in the empty air.
Between her toes
Tigris and Euphrates divide

and multiply. She loves you.
She loves you not.
Perhaps you are the pinprick rain

on the sheer face of an autumn lake.
Perhaps you are snow.
She is dreaming of crossroads

and you are the emptiness.
She is playing with dolls
and you are the mad muttering.

She is gossiping by the well
and you are the strewn fieldstones,
lidless eyes of the desert

waiting for rain. Her indecision
is delicious with cunning.
The mountains heave. Your leaves shiver.

When She Makes Mountains

she paints them shadow-dancing,
      rivers their flexions,
weaves the drapery wind. Dozes.

      Crosses into dream-space
with long-thighed stepping, her sleep-heat
      burnishing the low hills.

Out of them come women for water,
      bright as flowers, a dozen Salomes
with braceleted ankles and hard brutal feet

      who crouch on their haunches
under the thick scent of limes, their mud village
      creviced above them,

its brown face among the cliffs
      immobile as a blind man's.
She breathes them her gossip,

      whiskers their thighs,
puts the wheels of their hips
      in slow motion. Jars

grow from their heads, jars
      in the shape of women
heedless in May, the time of new grasses.

Sometime Before Words Perhaps

your arm moved—
a glitter of small hinges.
Or was it your leg,
its calculated unwinding?

I was asleep, say,
or lost in thought.
I heard your blood
though, how it sang,

and I felt your cloud-shadow
coming, crossing my face.
I looked—
you were full of yourself

dancing. I looked—
you were the waterfall of yourself
dancing. I looked—
your breath drank my eyes.

I listened—your feet drummed
shut my ears. I groped
but your skin turned fingers
to spider webs.
          Sometime,
out of the dark of my body
I spoke.

Today Perhaps the Lizard

who lies down in his own shadow,
inventing the sun through half-closed eyes,
feels his skin, thickening with years,
grow nervous as water.
Perhaps he just feels lucky.

You keep coming back like a dream.
Your hips make light shiver,
make me peer up silly-sideways
like an old dog
to watch the bonfire of your bones.

Night's coming, though.
The sky-blue water
of your eyes will turn dark
 then. Stars will come out.

Tomorrow
you will come and go again
like a river—
your bright bones
                    stealing my shadow.

At Twilight

Fatherless among the animals I wake in the half-light,
sinless as a June bug, pure as Narcissus.
I am what I look at.
The leaves see me and know my smell.
What I touch touches me back.

I cannot know whether I am the flower
or the flower of the flower
or just smooth water
reflecting tree more ravishing than tree,
flower more wayward than flower,

when your witch-light comes like gossamer
brushing my cheek.

Book VI:

FOR YOU I INVENT THE SUN

Where in this snow could I pick a rose for her

—Ghassan Zaqtan, "Other Conversations," trans. Fady Joudah

For You I Invent the Sun

1.
This, of course, is what money won't buy, this
hip-to-hip, two-centered circle, drift
and drift — you in front, provocative
as a pomegranate, me in front, hearing
echoes — your footsteps filling mine
the way perhaps snow fills the tracks
of caribou, keeping the wolves off. We're
birds of a feather. Our minds veer
and arc on the same air. It's open season here
on sun and wind, and I'm wearing my license
conspicuous and on my sleeve.

2.
We scuff and boot the leaves like six-year-olds,
grin like raccoons. *These are years,* we say,
shed like snake skins — doomed, irrelevant,
beautiful. Miles or years, we've walked
forever here, you and I, putting on
or shedding each other like light or leaves,
the traffic hushed and distant. We feel exotic
as the names of these lakeshore towns we walk in,
the water quiet, leaves falling, the light quixotic.
It's all new. You're new — taut and muscular
as a spring colt claiming his first field.
I'm new — grinning ear to ear, hearing windmills.
Death is new here, too, and moves like water underfoot.

3.
We drift in October light through the rose garden,
all the roses gone. Clothed in purple and black,
you're naked. Naked, raspberries and cream,
you're clothed. It's magic. For you I invent the sun,
feel tragic, drive it to your doorstep
in a long yellow cab, stand there, hat in hand,
like some foolish figure in a thirties' flick—

your hair darker than any back-row seat.

4.
You talk, stoop, pick weeds, say *the sky*
has breadth. I say birds have scissored
it to death, but I'm dazzled anyway.
It's late fall. The birds look hungrier.
You say you're leaving your husband anyhow—
for all his good, for all my bad.
Standing against a tree, your hood up,
your half-moon smile floating somewhere
below the hairline, I imagine you grew there
whole, yesterday perhaps, dew-like, and I
kiss you, feel shy, boyish — hungry
the way the old birds must
who won't get south.

5.
It's mid-winter and the crunching underfoot
sounds rare, precious. You're
purple and yellow. I'm fatigue L.L. Bean
gray green. The six years between us though
is hardly May and January,
and I'm dazzled by purple and yellow
and can outrun you anyway.
You admit now, though, cold hurts,
for all your tough talk. I should admit
what…for all my tough talk? — that my wife
writes, calls, cries, argues, accuses? Indeed
this crunching underfoot *is* precious — glass
or ice. It's January. It will soon
be May. Our rooms are white and beautiful
and bloom with plants.

6.
Your mother calls, sends chocolates, prays—
makes me feel like the anti-Christ. And
it's true enough I come from a land
of sand and stone, and never put much trust
in trees or green. (In my mind's eye
I always return

to the same rock ridge, almost abstract now
in the blind revision of its lie—
a dark sawblade raised against blue sky.)
But here, your walk is so much like the sun
or prayer, I must stoop
and touch the place you've stepped, knowing
come spring, something will grow there.

7.
Today bright sun makes blue sky and white birds
pure blue, pure white, barely visible
as we squint and almost stumble
in the pure light.
                        Yet we feel entitled here
as tourists, say, who've paid their fare,
though never dreaming it would look like this.
Beguiled by the low cant of foreign tongues,
we're half afraid some blunt truth in our own talk
will startle us back to earth, bring the dream
crashing like glass about our ears.
                                        But this
is mid-March,
                        when the wind blows and the domed sky
holds,
        when small nests of clustered stones
nosing into wind on the iced canal
rise and become birds.
                        This is the season
of the long white distance,
                                when seeing
is much like blindness, blindness like pure sight.

8.
You say, *You are the magician, I but the source.*
Who could top that? Who, mid-stride,
could help but feel the joy
of fear stutter his heart
like cloud-shadow. We have walked
a long time. It is growing dark. I wish
to take you in my arms. I wish to say
to the child we will one day make

You grew here, among sun and wind
in the gathering dark. I wish to say,
Your mother was taken
for goddess
among stones, among these circling
and calling birds,

                        and they were not far wrong.

9.
We have, I think, no word for this thin-aired
quiet full of light, through which we drift
like new ghosts
risen to Elysian Fields — the still, green lakes
somnolent as deep thought. It's the day
before Easter. The fishermen
standing on the firm bank
wave their fly-rods like bright wands
toward dark depths
where once new life must have climbed, sloth-like
into a dream of sunlight,
and where now loud children and willing dogs
are all smiles, wagging tongues,
sinew and muscle.
Today we talk less, think more.
Today we smile at all that is sensuous
and literal.

Trees

Today they've come back from the snow—
their dream-walk that began in December—
and are settling in along the ravine
where the creek runs, shaking the fatigue
from their bones, talking softly among themselves.
In a week the elders will speak in tongues.
In two they'll be chanting.
Muskrat will hum.
In a month the blue flower of the lake
will break from her icy spell.

Fog

We woke
to cathedrals
of fog — spires, robes, angels—
valhallas of choral voiced silence.
Its breath obliterated farms,
rode the lake's abyss like a warship.
It took the antlers of trees as its standards.
It marched north along roads
whose cars blundered over ridges
like sleepy cattle. Crocuses
brightened like tiny suns
in the sulfurous galaxies of mosses.
On the second day, it lost pomp and contour.
Drum-silent, it lay moiling over hills in listless aftermath.
It clung to our eye-corners like sooty laundry.
By the third day, the tittering of birds was strange.
Their calls vibrated through invisible holes in our bodies.
Our mouths hung stupidly open — our eyes
merely the shifting mirrors of fog. Our hearing
crept out over fields without hope or longing.

The Mountain

The mountain
at the south gateway
of our glacier lake (still white as satin
in late March) is more glorified hill
than mountain,
                    but with the sullen blue presence
of mountain, a sort of brow ridge
thrust up from the softer brown thighs
of the other hills—
                    bouldered in Pleistocene sleep,
a hill, like Cezanne's, a man
could walk around for years
and get lost in, his eye cutting
narrow goat paths of perfect
clarity.
        So hill becomes mountain
in a vibration of eye waves, in the forgetting
of tedious plains thrust up out of
sea bottom shiftlessness—
                    leans hard
in the wind, poised toward some moment
it has lost all track of.

Geese

Over hills russetted by late sun
and the silent underfires of hard winter
the geese rise.

They rise over yesterday's white lake,
today a sudden fiery blue,
into coppery, blood-thirsty, perfect sky.

Suddenly I understand their struggle with sun—
It is a wound, their wound. They are bathed in blood
as they rise, necks craned, shuffling, regrouping,

finding their bearings, gathering the sun's power
into their left eye and along their immaculate, outstretched
identical bodies, while below them

the jesterings of black birds in twos and threes
ape their gigantic herding, tittering
at the titanic effortings, swooping and plunging

but wishing them well—or not well
but farewell. While I, chilled and breathless,
take my own chance in the last light

and dance with the oldest tree
on my property, a twisted old apple, all elbows
and shudderings, beaks and talons, a crone

of unparalleled eloquence and elongations,
simperings and croonings, a cackling
of refracted lights and reddening shawls,

burnt siennas, rising as the geese rise
and dancing to the goose's song
until the geese are gone.

March Invitation

Today every tree
a hand of withheld fire,
twisted and passionate against the sky—

Rain back to snow, indecisive,
gusts into a sleety, crow-battering wind
combing lusterless scraggy hills,

sifting the sick fields — loam-scent
rising like a witch-brew elixir
from the crushed pterodactyl skull
of last year's robin.

O ravenous mouth making trees shiver,
the black hearts shudder—

If they knew the glad-hand light of summer
working them like a politician full of promises,
how could they forget in their slag-sleep
this whispery touch, this tingling wakefulness
under the dark dreaming magma of sky?

But their amnesia grows perfect again—
O schoolgirls in the hands of the March wind!

I See You Bend Down

in the garden of pain, the garden of spring,
your after-frost loam-blackened fingers
rooted in roots, dreaming the furred shoots
and delicate unfoldings
of dewy lipped angels attuned to the stars,

and some jungle in me starts growing,
some man of leaves gone slitty-eyed
with cunning, who scans the sky
for a new pale moon

to catch tonight
in the arms of the hairy
old forest—
         dark mangrove, tall cypress.

He Just Walked Out

slouched into the dark in his big black body
and did not come back. His fine-furred ears
fluttered as usual at the night's touch.
He slunk slowly down each wet step,
tail testing the air-chills, coiled
at the first touch of grass, then shape-shifted
into the black.
                He was something to look at,
Bagheera in miniature, with the subtlest
coppery rivers cascading through the black
forest of fur, eyes saffron-speckled
in a dark tiger's face
from a fairy tale.
              He slept lordly in the sun
on the couch back, or dangled his tail-tip
over the edge for the puppies to swat,
needling them back with a single extended claw
glinting daggerish from a black velvet glove.
Or rolled on his back and taught all five or six
from each litter, for years, the delicate art
of disembowelment.
              He had humor it seemed,
or even something like love's patience
when he snaked his way among the lewd lumps
of our sleep, to nag us back gently
from the forest of dreams to the sharp-scented
fact of his cat bowl.
              But he was never ours
any more than the wind or the bird cries.
He'd come back bloodied and satisfied
after days on his own, sleep a day
and a half, and then wake with kittenish
cuddliness.
              We'd taken his testicles,
the jewels of his most absolute being,
so it was not entirely the treacherous
lure of sex that drove him, but perhaps

sex sublimated into the godhead night,
lure of star and shadow, death-cries,
life-pulse, drew him to the black edge
of himself,
          and now I feel him gone,
eyes lusterless and receding among
the hundred similar dead eyes of spring.
He walked out on Good Friday.
Easter brought us the first real spring.
A pair of sparrows is nesting in the small
juniper so close to the house
they too must know he's gone.
I walk out to feel the night air's
soft indifference, to relish its furred face.
What I call my property is being divvied up
differently tonight, fur and feather and bone
in the twisted paths of moonlight.
The bright eyes laugh, winking across the lake.
The stars dive one by one to drown
and be reborn.
          And everywhere whispers
in the telepathy of time and distance:
the cat, the cat.

Hawk

Dark-rumored inkling of air-chills,
pulsing pupils, the whole hill
monastery-still, a tilting
cliff's edge empty
reckoning — blue water, blue sky.

Ponderous, as if in chains,
attended by black birds, he rises
out of the tree-fringe
hoisted by huge shoulders, granite facemask
blank as an angel's

over the flapping canopy of lake
unwavering and undeterred, past lake rim and horizon
into miraculous high noon
where he who owns nothing, not shadow or hunger,
absolves utterly,

becomes nothing—all shadow, all hunger—
the eye-scorching sun unmasked in its bottomless plummet.

Solstice

This afternoon green, angel-winged, shimmering
summer is upon us, a solemn shadowed, silky
sibilant rejoicing of gnats and dragonflies
in heart-throb stillness.

Only the purr of her engines, in full throttle,
disrupts the fish-silence of stars, the Scheherazade
dawn-silvering, moon-mingling, dusk-moiling
blossom of the lake, my son's face

rapt in the reflected bauble of the world.
We fall down like the stars and we die
mutters the machinery of the green woods,
inventing the full weight of the sun,

its canopied light, wing-pulse murmurings.
We rain down like the sun
                              and he smiles, he smiles.

Raccoon

Days past death, he was decomposing
in a ditch by the roadside,
body gossamered by maggots,
haloed by shed, fine fur,
the black swoon of his limbs
grease for the black oil of earth,
his head no longer head
but the mask of an angel's
upward gaze, the shrunk hands
supplicant.
        Out of the murderous
innocence of midnight, he'd come
strolling, with hands of a jewel thief,
eyes of a gypsy — knocked dead
in a moment.
        The dawn did not mourn him
but lit up the last silvering of his pelt.
The crows pecked at him and savored his eyes.
The maggots swarmed him.
All that pilfering would end soon.
By morning, the curved struts of his keel bone
would house only wind crossing
the leeching black ooze of his emptiness.

Passage

Into the shadows and a little beyond,
your dream — leaping black dancers
burying the sun,
                              low river absence.
O lost sad body
of ruined chances, gone-vague
rumor of home.
                              Into the stone
silence of bones, under the archway of light,
come agony of alder, oath of oak,
solemn presage of elders—
                              to the bagpipe drone
of the smoke-boned mosquito, dancing the tangible sun.

Nightwood

The dogs tell me they've come,
a skin crawling, fur bristling,
alert, faces in the moonlight
statuary stillness, pressuring
a slight yelp from the youngest.

Something come down in the midnight
from behind the hill's eyelid
travels with the patience of the blind,
browses and peers in at us
with unearthly eyes, as though

the lights of our house were hellfire
guarded by wolves, a terror
that lures them out of slow chewing
sidelong glances, flickering
uncertainty, sudden hoof-thump

oaken vigilance—something more near
than heartbeat, but older, antlered,
waist-deep in the sky-deep blackness,
eyes shining perhaps like stars,
ghosts older than the Iroquois

turned back into trees by the dawn.

Always

under the leaves there was death waiting,
despite your tuned, high-voltage body.

Tigers and rivers glide in us nameless
though the day fades and it is never enough.

The poem deconstructing was an old saw
but we made honey in its warm caldron

and I said *love* with the white mouth
of the moonflower, with iridescent suns

of coneflowers flaunting whispery black eyes.
It was summer in the garden where you moved

without burden of self like a cloud, paused,
looked, shifting your glorious haunches

like any happy horse claiming its field—
all heat and hunger and applause.

Nightscape

The lake tonight is river in the sultry south,
still, smoky, under insect chirr
and black, swampy boughs. A single dock light
claims its lance of silver water
that means loneliness, or hope, or beauty's
steely, soft indifference to beauty.
Out there the old river is speaking to no one
and no one is listening. The half moon
rising is pure Islam.
                            Even my bones
know
        wherever they are is home.

Diffusions of August

Somewhere, I think, there lurks a poem today—
aching perhaps on the horizon
or in the lost last blue sky of summer.

"I stay indoors and spoil another season"
wrote the old master,
searching the moment within a moment

when the present fades
and there is only the present—
to walk forth crippled thereafter.

Bless us with this curse lisp the thick leaves
with their fat shadows, sibyls
of midnight, silvery wombs of the morning.

The spidery breeze on my face
has come its thousand miles.
The tall trees honor me.

I walk among mountains
and know the angels' names.
I drag my lame foot and feel the beggar's shame.

"They want me to wear old clothes...
not walk in the painted sunshine...
but live in the tragic world."

Hail to thee, dark talkers,
shakers of leaves,
whispering still in the soft air,

in the lazy air,
as insects rattled in the golden blaze
when the poem got made.

Scoffers

This morning a wide-fingered hand
crossed the hood of my car
like a great ray — undulant, ghostly,
more mind-shadow across adobe wall
than simple crow wing's sudden dark
against the metal sheen.
                              Later,
shadowy among trees, their calling
unnerved me, creaking like oarlocks,
and their flapping, eavesdropping absences
pestered my eye-corners — laughter
like bitten off blood-oaths
flung loveless to summer skies, undermining
even the jeweled lichens, the great cascading
cliffs of leaves.
                      And now in a boggy valley
atop the mast-high skeletons of elms,
they cluster like thieves on yardarms
or the tattered crest-plumes of buried horsemen
come back over deathless snows
to claim the purple of loosestrife,
psalming greens of the rushes—
the pinwheel turnings of death's rainbow
in each small, malevolent eye.

Pilgrimage
— in memory of Roland Lombard, DVM

I have entered the circle of old men.
They are "talking dogs" and I have been invited.
Outside in the October chill, the dogs are restless.
We hear their chains jingling, sense their feet
quick-dancing, their new fur rippling and attentive.
We know their Asiatic eyes are bright as stars
after first snow — they who come from a world
with 200 words for snow.
                              Inside, the first man speaks.
He has a womanizer's easy smile, a slaver's hard laugh.
He's run with the best and beaten them.
He tells of being chased by wolves, a panicky jab
of a ski-pole into the haunch of a dog
suddenly crouched and frightened — the yelp,
the burst of speed. He tells of later
fastening that ski-pole to the sled frame
just at dog eye-level, banishing forever
the big gray's shrewd laziness.
                              The next
draws slow on a cigarette, speaks slow,
tells of 1400 miles of Antarctic wastes,
crevasses opening like grim mouths, nails
digging in for dear life, the sheer guts,
tirelessness, even the autocratic Byrd's
grudging admiration, despite their small frames.
He smiles then and waits for the third
                              who cannot speak
but has eyes like blue fires, wolf's eyes
under shaggy white brows — patient, fierce,
yet mild in their singleness of purpose.
That he can no longer speak seems proof
he's gone hunting with wolves, entering
their silence like a furred, ghostly god.
He is legend even among the Inuit
for kindness, for indefatigable attention
to detail, able to enter a dog's mind

and bring out the best with no more
than a cluck or gesture — who's felt the wind
of the bull moose charging, the white bear's
shadow, yet come back again and again
to beat the best of the younger men.
It is this quiet the dogs outside are restless for,
his quick signal the hunt is on.
                                He has fashioned
a model of scapula, humerus and radius/ulna
to show me the shoulder blade's proper rotation.
Outside, he buries my hands in the deep ruff of his leader,
his eyes searching mine for the flicker of comprehension.
Each dog, whirling on its chain like a separate constellation,
keeps eyes riveted on him, waiting for the touch,
the nod, the gesture.
                        A gasp goes up
as we stare into the treacherous ravine that starts
his training trail, now over half a century old.
"He wants to die on the runners," someone whispers.
The first stars have come out, their light perhaps
even colder than wolf's eyes. A hint of snow's
in the air, but also a surge, electric, similar
to a February night I stepped from a Lakota sweat lodge
and stared into buffalo fire—
                        the horned skull
speaking to the stars.

Ghost Moon

haunted by cries on a November afternoon.
The geese, with their compass needle necks,
their tumultuous hurry

are passing, have been passing
for days. Each with a piece of magnetic field
planted deep behind its sun-fired eye

heading south. Jostled by wind, pelted
by rain. *Unlikely, unlikely*
their cacophonous holler, their harpy wail.

Something of us goes with them,
feels the ebb in the blood tides
and salt marshes, the emptiness, the cold.

Ceremony

Tonight black skeletons of maples against a November sky
is all I know of heaven and all I hope to know.
Russell Means is dead. Geronimo is dead. Crazy Horse
is dead. And in the land of the sacred outlaw
Obama has taken the White House.
Viva Zapata and his white horse.
Viva the snake-eyed killers of lies
and those who stand in line.

Tonight under the long ache of distance and far stars,
I celebrate ghosts whose moccasined soles
listened to earth, the great mystery of trees,
coyotes yelping on a black hill.

The Road Home, November

Twilight needling the eye — the fogged out,
whited out road collapsing
into goblin namelessness, withering
weird trees, half-light lure
of dog and deer
in the treacherous bearded fields—

Giving in to centuries-old, no-world silence—
head down, nape-of-the-neck
bristling attention
to far star-cauldron nothingness—

Papery-skulled, haggard
from the hard-voiced night,
I come to myself
building a fire — webby, ochre light,
oily shadows, elemental
stonehenge geometry of logs, inscrutable
as the star-crossed bones of bison
bruise-blotting the clammy walls of caves.

Later my son's raw edged ancient crying
and soft-haired nuzzling.

Among Mushers
—in memory of Charlie Belford, DVM

There is something old and beautiful
about the great dog men of the snow—
cussed, crafty as they are
about their tricks of trade.
Trickery is for them serious business
sacred to the dog god as to the wolf god,
confessed, years later, in mock-serious tones—
slow smiles spreading across granite faces.
Young and fierce, they kept the silence
of snow, the blood-oaths of black cold.
Their hands are scarred like fishermen's or farmers'.
They'll trust a good dog before a good man
and a good woman before either.
They share the broke bones and blood sagas
of bull riders. What saved them was a dog
or their wits, or some goddamned good luck.
What you feel, even if you're not one of them,
is flint and fire, laughter out of cold stars.

Dead of Winter

Old one, I have seen your vacant eye.
It was all night sky, a lens of stars.
From the myrtle of my imagination
I made myrrh and the forest scent
of the new moon, the slow columns of light—
winter there in the trees, in the soft
heavy deaths of the snows.

New snow is the light-pealed crystal
of longing winking dead stars, the inlaid,
still swirling trunks of trees etched in ebony,
precisely feathery as a photographer's negative.
It says I am not here with my daylight eyes,

I have come trackless and scentless
as a mirage to this blanche
of purest silver, this black-river calm.
Old stars move in my veins.
I have seen reflected in your eye, old one,

the interminable dead light in the live deer's shadow
and fires flickering in a far field.

A Moment in February

It is the light at the center of every cell.
　　　　—Mary Oliver

See how the silky sun floods the ermine fields—
ton on ton of sheer white light
tumbling kid-gloved soft — each sun-swooned tree
transfixed, snow mittened, bowed as in prayer.
These are the plains of Xanadu
tilting skyward, the high steppes of the Horseman.
Or this is upstate New York shaken
by the vast pastness of the heart, journeys leading nowhere
but here — sun on the snow, the slurred fur
of feel. And everywhere, tremulous, a shout

that's only the sunlight
ringing the molten hearts of trees.

Remains

My son guides me up the long hill
squelching in run-off, along trails
narrow as goat paths through the trees
to show me the strewn bones of a deer
nested in her shed shreds of fur,
almost golden, where some wood spirit
laid her to rest, and the coyotes
and crows stripped her, leaving only
a hoof and furred knuckle intact
among a clutter of collapsed ribs.
He shows me the clean white vertebrae,
the pelvis with its odd eye hole,
the knee still attached with some last rope
of sinew.   This is his find, stumbled on
as he tried his new spring legs in a downhill,
helter-skelter run, and stopped, and stared,
and in his eleven-year-old mind knew
that this was the stuff of running
undone, something the receding snow
left for him personally, a sign
of winter's weight.   We eye it together.
We go down on our knees to gather pieces
of the witchcraft mystery. The gray trees
around us are also bones that click
and chatter in the wet wind
of almost spring. The brown limpid eyes
are gone. The crumbling gnarl
of spine, once nerved and tremulous,
is now only a train wreck the grass
will hide in a month's time. We feel
the doorway of earth opening.
We feel the thinness of our skins
and the prickling of short hairs rising.

We know what's at the bottom of things,
how soon the mayflies will be dancing
their measured reels of the evening.

His Mountain Gateway
—for Will Hier

All day death hovered—
coming through weeks of the gray of November—
becoming the friend
who would not last the year

and did not last the week.
The lake of his dream
became a fuming of crystals
and polished obsidian.

The cold deepened and the ice whistled
and the lake thundered
and the scarred ice vanished
and the whitecaps foamed

till spring became a reflection
of olive placidity, browns
transforming to the delicate
hairy greens

of a thousand shades and nuances
before the leaf-loaded abundance
of summer dreamed
purple evenings etched in shadow,

his photographer's eye
honing beauty out of the hard edges
of weather, season
after season drawn on the lens.

And in the long view south
the mountain named for Song
at the gateway between two mountains
that told us we were home—

the gateway
where I imagine him still—

his farmer's trudge—
bull shoulders, dexterous hands—

casting a warm
but slightly squint eye
on life, on death,
and passing by.

Over Dinner We Begin to Vanish

Let me not to the marriage of true minds
Admit impediments.
—Shakespeare

The faces behind our conversation
begin to sag.
In hard light we look bad.
We know what was.
We laugh.
Soon knowing won't matter
and the moon will rise.

      *   *   *

The moon will rise
into the twin
obsidian lakes of midnight,
one water, one sky, owls
chuffing their bloodlusts. Two pools
suddenly bottomless
will wake in one another's morning.

      *   *   *

We'll wake in one another's morning
with Coyote's cunning,
Raven's black laugh,
a whole day to do mischief,
shuffle the sign, bend the law,
eons to rearrange
the faces behind our conversation.

River Time

The hills are green with summer,
the lakes cobalt blue and glittering.
Whatever we longed for in March
is here already or forgotten.
Your hair gleaming obsidian
as always, despite a few white renegades,
your body stretches out like a great cat's
or a landscape I never tire of crossing.
When I kiss the small of your back,
I hear the whisper of desert sands,
the rush of young rivers. No one comes back.
No one steps twice in the same body.
Spring was sun on the daffodils
and the time of the new wide sky,
the heart-breaking golds
of the giant willows.
Marry me, marry me
shouted the cardinal in his tall tree
while the goldfinch giggled
I am nothing but light.

Spring Haiku

Easter
in the purple
tulip tree
blooms
gold finch
yellow laughter—
zoom

* * *

Zoom—
yellow laughter
gold finch
blooms
tree tulip
in the purple
Easter

The Woods

(*Going to the woods is going home*—John Muir)

Each spring we dream our return—
brown floor of leaves
framed by fiery new green
welcoming us to our animal deaths,

bones picked clean
by teeth and weather,
shadows
among the walking trees,

insect song,
to curl up with ferns
in the mulch of a thousand
deaths and entrances

before the path thickens and darkens
and closes in
and the jungle of August

bars the way.

Book VII:

BEFORE SPEECH

Tired of all who come with words, words but no language
I went to the snow-covered mountain.
The wild does not have words...
I come across the marks of roe-deer's hooves in the snow.
Language but no words.

—Tomas Transtromer, "From March '79"

Before Speech

was the wolf pack, the moon's children,
her insignia borne in the whites of their faces.

There was high ground at the heart of their forest
sacred for long sight, steeped in their smells.

There was bow and gesture, a sniff of the ear
that meant home, that meant heart,
that meant abiding mother with her belly in the dirt.

There was signal flashed across space.
There was the will to sing.
Anyone could start.

Alien

Dropped here from outer space,
her eyes infrared scanners,
she wants to be fed and for the world
to go away. She wants to grow feathers
for her star-cruiser
body to glide the rivers of blackness
she'll come to call home.
In her spaceship egg, she was a whole
galaxy, a liquid listening.
Soon she'll learn about the particle snow,
stealing its white loveliness
as her cold cover. Soon she'll learn about death
under the covenant of stars,

but she will call it life,
chanting her flute-songs of exile.

Squandered by the Hundred Millions

his hell-hunks of rotting flesh
left to slough from his bones
like sacrifices to the god of steel,

one and one and one
he died, she died, they all died,
their stunned unreckoning

rose into stars, numberless as stars.
And the night came
lifting him up with his black rage

and gave him back his magical curving horns,
and lifted his mountainous woolly back-skull
onto the still larger mountains of black woolly shoulders,

and polished his small black eyes
and sharp hooves, his thunderous black bones,
and patched his scraggy, reeking beard.

But by morning the tractors had come
and the grasses vanished, and the dust came,
and that was the end of the first day.

Scales

Old bubble brain
floating in primordial ooze—
Turn him on his back
and he sinks into coma,
forgets yesterday, hardly fathoms
tomorrow.

How easily we condescend
in our neocortical glimpse.
He cannot laugh or be sociable.
His one purpose
to go on expanding, to eat
and be filled and eat again.

Mountain ranges grow from his back.
His each scale anticipates
the iron age by eons.
He is the Hindu calendar
written in Braille.
For him it's still the beginning of time.

Expressionless as God.
His undulant tail
the shadowy frond of some first fern
the abstract angels dance on.

Beluga

What were once perhaps arms have simplified in time
to water wings, undulant and white in a black sea
pearled and catacombed with ice.
                              Pelvis has vanished,
or is at most vestigial, tapering to feet turned tail fin
in a slow fan of somnolent propulsion,
dream-lazy, ghostly.
                        Her call, her only weapon,
is sonar deadly, a stun gun, prelude
to instant swallowing and digestion, death
under anesthetic.
                        The world of stars and sun
and the hard crust of earth
betrayed her, though she visits still,
white in the white moonlight—
                              the dome of her mind
grown huge and forgiving in the cave of the sea.

Taking It Slow

Methuselah in his mudpack paradise
cools his scales in ooze
and peers out from beneath his dome
in utter indifference:
a world so changed from his youth,
so withered, so shrunken,
he dreams he carries it on his back,
blinking in the slow sun—
lipless, mute as stones or the far stars.

Amazons

A pride of 30 lionesses — single
pre-phalanx wall of blond muscle,
pure infantry — slides in one hunger
through the one darkness, patient
as desert wind, insect heat—
slides motionless as the deep sea
stone minded in its one dream
rivered with tendons.
                              What awaits this
in the brush, in the shadow burrows
and ruts of the night wind, must dream
mouths larger than prairies, frieze
in the moonlight nameless as stars
falling — impala become Impala, warthog
Warthog, its riveting shrill shriek
a shearing of metal—
                              night erupting
into bonfire — claws, teeth, flesh,
kin and carcass — mandarin faces,
sleeked in blood, scarred senile
in the anarchy of kill.

Later they'll greet the dawn,
lolling, licking each other, satisfied
they've kept the universe open,
the tall dead rising.

So Close to the Edge

of his granite, glacier-sheared promontory,
the claws of his massive forepaws
overhang it—
          shoulders, neck, and doleful wedge head
riding the abyss—
            a siren song, wind's nocturne,
the bitter soul's hungering departure.
                All of him goes into it
and upward
until he is only the vanishing host of a voice—
an open question in a Zen listening—
              calling and calling.

Tiger Dance

She is the languid, languorous
disease of the sun, flower
of his passion, hint
of his corruption among shadows.

He comes to her disguised
as her double, only larger,
more impossibly brutal-beautiful—
his face a Paleolithic sun shower.

She in turn turns tiger lily,
all smiles and pussycat frailty
shivery under his touch—
needier, whorier

than his lewdest imaginings—
his great winking anus
laughing at the winking
gay forest above them.

This is he who has hugged
and scarred the trees
as his vassals, whose gape
at her nape is the very vault of heaven.

This is she
who releases him,
brings on the darkness,
leaves him free again to love nothing.

Black Leopard

Where she comes down

in a slow boil
of uncoiling muscles,
dropping the last few feet

onto spongy big feet,
rosette points
like black stars on a black river—

we know this place,
deep in our sleep,
moonlight silvering the ancient leaves,

the scarred, inscrutable
dream-mask, ears
like small delicate flowers.

The baboon barks once and is still.
The sambur shift and stamp
in the rasping, dry grass.

They too know the myths of the death tree
and the death shadow, of distant yellow suns
smoldering in the furred midnight.

The Great Mother, After Long Drought

so tiny eyed, so tired, so wrinkle-rivered
in her skin of dust,
has trudged so long in billowing skirts of dust,
knelt fat-assed and humbled as Old Mammy
in chasms of dust—
her great trumpeting trunk following its long instinct
for water.

Now she has come. Leading her cows
into the kingdom of cows,
down long winding rivers of cows,
single-file, dust-smoldering processions—
tusked, vigilant, thunder-shaking—
meeting and touching each
to each in the great milling of cows.

Such soft-handed knowing in that fondling
probing lip! Such fingertip-tender
tickling laughter
behind the preposterously old faces—
Even *elephant* is not word enough!

The rivers are jubilant!
The mud holes grow deeper!
She has come
like a black cloud
bringing a black cloud
to a land like her very skin!

Earth shaker! Bellower! Maker of rain!

Mother of Angels

is dreaming her web—
swings through the firmament
with electron purpose,
trembling feelers—
                        minute mindless astronaut
at her gadgetry, each leg
a violin string
tendering a single blood-note,
each eye
many-eyed with malice—
                        Little Alice
of ice
dangling her lace curtain,
humming primly to her ribbon,
throbbing in the open air
like a suddenly ripped out
heart
      alive to nerve twitches,
death-shouts—
                        herself the toneless ticking
of her eggs.

The Serval, Demure as Nefertiti

can swat down the startled thunder
of a guinea cock
a full six feet in air,

her face in feathers
as behind a Chinese fan.
Long glamorous legs, ears plucking sound

from tiniest twig whisper,
she paints herself into the scrub
with pointillist self-effacement,

still as death for hours.
Or rolls the bowls of her muscles
in hair-trigger readiness.

No mirror-reflecting waywardness—
No hum of thought in the taut strings of her body—
Sloe-eyed gleaming guardian of the field's sleeplessness.

One Paw Poised

the others planted in snowpack,
here is the lost spirit of the moon's cunning,
joy of the hunt, joy of the kill—

who claimed the gothic conifers
before Goths or Vandals
or the Westward Expansion—

who felt the steel trap's
bodiless jaws, the bullet's
invisible fang; twisted in strychnine

bewilderment—
hung upside down
on iron crosses of barbed wire

and died by the myriad
for our sins.
           Now let us praise him.

Black Wolf at Midnight
(after the print by Robert Bateman)

At first we do not see the eyes—
bewitched, bewitching — only trees,

their latticework of iced branches
glittering where moonlight patches

the dark, where any moment centuries
old stone cold silence threatens

to crack like ice the thin bark
in the eternal click, click

of minerals in the soft shift of wind.
Some moccasined tracker in skins

crouched under stars, cold heart
in his mouth, might have stared out

and seen, for the first time,
the colossal foot — hairy, snow-rimed—

planted too eerily close. Dread
paw of the wolf feathering upward

to where the gray column of leg dwarfs
the wrist-thick trunks of the light-starved

trees. Then fathomless bulk
of black body and mystic gold

eyes latched onto him there in that
first dark. Ours is the more distant

wonder of Art, that he could do this
so stealthily, shrewdly, our eyes

tuned to these eyes, our gaze
fixed to this stare without remorse

or malice, a criminal angel's—
our shadow brother lost in the ages

light years after.

Wolf Song

I return to the river,
my tail plume light as a feather
in feathery wind.
I am the stones' ancestral voices.
I am the wide earth listening.

My girl is my playmate
in a song of Hafez,
quick feet to feed our children,
eyes the color of spring rivers.
See our big tails dancing!

Red sky. Rock ridge. So I travel
and the gold sun honors me,
singer of high places, queen night,
sifter of pheromones.
I scent the leaves and my good bones marvel—

lordly in the far off
nearness, the arrow and the bow.

Book VIII:

DISPOSSESSED CREEDS
AND BROKEN CODES

Artists are the Indians of the white people.

—Lame Deer

Mon Semblable, Mon Frère
for K.S.K.

Old Oily Bones crouching in the Ganges' mud
or sauntering up our drive, Tequila and peppers
proffered like flowers, I feel your shadow
lurking in corners months after you depart—
broken-down Caddy asputter.
                              We drink late,
spout poems and oaths, feel the sun rise
through bleached bones, know the same curse
blesses as the stones are blessed, as Tequila is blessed
and the tongue is a shrine.
                              We swell with the pride
of Flamenco swagger, ride the old blues uncouth
truth and parody, feel the universe
slide through us.
                    You're gone in a swill of rucksacks
and vagabond luggage, crazy patois,
leaving us waving down the drive.
                              The day
 is full of patches of sun, on the counter,
across the desk, shadows in the gold grass,
as I feel you retreating
                          back into the tall Pennsylvania timber,
head down, long strides, back into the long silence
of unmade poems and gypsy songs.

Reading Heaney

No need to get carried away the voice
says meaning there'll be time enough for that
.
life anyway a slow leak back into
stars from that first edge-of-the-world place

bog-rooted and hedged in cow-quivering sleet
and the imperative to keep weather out

along with such novelties and courtesies
and verities of tongue as horse traders use

language come up to look men in the eye
across the pasture gate and slow reticence

of educated hands attaching fact
to fact all the way back to the Bog Woman

in her death necklace—
                              though the boy looks out
enthralled by the imperative of dawn

to stop thinking to start it all again—
hear the poem knotted up in the sheep's bleat

or the valley's clattering first hooves of light

Drum Song
—in memory of Ted Hughes

The lightning-flashed hag face of the moor
in the torpor of downpour
and the drizzle-dim skull of Heptanstall

and the curse in the blood of the cursed mud
and Heathcliff's Mother-wound horror
put thistle in the tongue of Yorkshire

the crashing shires and long haul of mountains
where rock and wind ate at each other
and ached for each other like star-crossed lovers

fossilized in poems whose undersong
was the silkiest hands of farmers
coaxing at the womb door

and the galloping gaiety of the otter
slipping his pelt like a sorcerer
and the river's unkillable contradictions and seasons

her unkillable children and thunder

in the big double drum of the heart

Eros/Thanatos   Eros/Thanatos   Eros/Thanatos.

Lowell

In the old New York, we said
"If life could write,
it would have written like us."

You lost your arid God, His dragon tail
and gorgeous plumage whipping the sea swell
of your Promethean will and thunder
in your "all percussion" obit for the Quaker—
manner or matter your evolving question—
the boy-Keats muscled to the nearly German.

What then? The down look and the letting go,
whiskey glazed eye in false-gold afterglow,
the soft patter of friends no longer pattering,
snippets, smatterings,
crisscrossed conscience and coincidence,
the world's crush
crumpling in a handkerchief—
as if the daze of old age were all day
in a deckchair's decadent complicity
or child's play.

I like the last poems best, their blurry wonder
and disconnects…
the Boston Brahmin with the southern drawl,
vernacular still sparring for the jugular…
the convalescent back from rehab…
seafarer
come home in a New York cab.

Talkin' Bob's Blues

You can't get there from here though you can go a lot of places
In the switchyard of the mind you can rearrange a lot of faces
But the scent of her hair and the touch of her lips and the curse of
                                                              her tongue
Say you'll bleed from your eyes till the day you're done

When the plains' red dawns stretch out like lies
And the cut glass of the past gives you spider web eyes
And you feel like you're crawling through the land of the dead
And know the dream of your life should have stayed home in bed

And you don't wanna do what beauty asks
Though she's always there in the mirror's masks
Jean Genet in the role of town crier
Or the vagabond king disguised as vampire

Or the ragamuffin boy who could be anyone
Hank or Woody or the scourge of the sun
Deranging the world to see for the first time
Mississippi was a state of mind
And Desolation just a street sign

You can't get there from here though you jump through hoops
You can dance on the clouds or you can deal from the stoops
Your mama had a sister her sister had a friend
She wanted to bust out he wanted to keep it in
And a baby's cry is the willow's wind
You can't even pray without some kind of sin

Walk down the backstairs slip off in the dark
The devil's face is Joan of Arc's
We might be 40 miles outside of somewhere
But the locals say you can't get there from here

Smoke's been travelin' all through the swamps
Says the trees have been whisperin' the words of *Mein Kampf*
Innocence cries in even the darkest heart

You can die for a rose or you can die for art
And all kinds of things that were wrong from the start

I got a woman behind my door
Says she'll love me but I gotta be poor
Gotta crawl on my knees gotta howl like a dog
But if I'm a prince she'll make me a frog

You can't get there from here though you toss and you turn
And your dreams get heavy and your eyes start to burn
But there's a place you can get to on down the road
Where lying's just another kind of truth in code

And an old man playing a Chinese flute
Says I've had mine you can take the loot
The white beard of nothingness grows from my chin
And the next time we meet we'll all be kin

There's a place I go about a mile from here
Where I take off my face and examine my fear
The lake shines like a mirror and I cup my ear
And nothing much matters but that the words are clear

There are freight cars passing and old crossroads
And dispossessed creeds and broken codes
And dead end dreams where a life implodes
And sometimes you see her dancing in fire
But you can't sing her back from the land of desire

You can bray like a donkey you can caw like a crow
There are some kinds of places words can't go
He went down in the valley to sing his song
And let the echo decide if he was right or wrong

He let the echo decide if he was right or wrong

Vilnius Glimpses

For Kornelijus Platelis

In the lonely room of the poem

(sifting
plaster dust
and spreading wall
maps of moisture
in the slow
garlic-sour crumble
of old Europe)

the heavy-faced poet ponders the book of losses
dreaming redemption
from the irony and ache of arthritis

or maybe the clatter and clash of sun-bright weapons
as the pagan suicide knights of the forest
vanish into the blood-smoke incense
of the crucifix

but no let up in the relentless walk of the world
eyes dead ahead
ghosts of the mind cops and word killers

and too little mystery or amnesia
in a quart of *degtine*

no matter the glassy glitter of boutiques
no matter the smart fashion-girls with their cell phones
and small taut buttocks

and the roaring poets of cavernous taverns
blinking into the sun
to mumble poems like apologies
in the still sacred tongue of oak and linden

and placating shrines to the gothic gods of unmaking—
rampant St. George plunging
his lance into the waiting mouth of the monster
and interchangeable saints
wilting like flowers

I want to go home to make love
to my beautiful wife
on the timeless hill of our dreams
stolen from the Iroquois

I want to tear out my teeth in the soundproof
torture chambers of the KGB
and forget the cool-eyed women cut down
in the demystified forest
like a thousand Dianas

I want words to unsay themselves
and the clocks to stop

I want to drink till I drop
and sleep in the gutter
with the rain leaking into my brain
and be washed in the blood
of inscrutable gutturals
and make a friend of sorrow and terror

I don't want to be written into the heavy book
of the poet with his bitter grief
and Sphinx-like gaze
knowing it all might have been otherwise

though our eyes have met
and there's no going back

A Dream of Falling
—in memory of Karl Wallenda

He slept perhaps
the way Sherpas
on a long climb
sleep: on the move,
as though the mountain
were mere dream and the next step
all that mattered: a hole
pushed into the nothing
that it might vanish
into nothing
and leave him to wake refreshed.

He woke to a dream
of falling. If there was a scream
it came from another room. It was not
his. He was too transfixed
to scream. He had dreamed the dream
too often.
       But then he had not come
to conquer the mountain. He had done that
years ago: wooed it and brought it to his bed
like a woman. Now he came to the mountain
as a mountain, and dreamed of a man
falling, a man gone suddenly womanish
and expansive, opening his body to sky,
accepting it, as the mountain does, with open arms.

Book IX:

INVOCATIONS

Like him, we too have eaten of the word:
with him are somewhere lost beyond the Gorge:
and write, in rain, a letter to lost children,
a letter long as time and brief as love.

—Conrad Aiken, "A Letter from Li Po"

Invocations

My steps slower than I would have imagined
even in summer

who once could not help but run
Crimes I've done myself I would not undo

Cicadas in a tree singing
the dappled 'out there'

the shrill of birdsong
*   *   *   *
Sands of the desert and sun warm me
and I forgive my pederast father
and remember his shy laugh

Spawn of East Texas swamps snakes on the brain
Stink of rot and piney woods loneliness
Bible-belt mom dowsed in lavender

I had an engineer's hat like my grandfather's
high in the sun-flared locomotive squinting into the light

the two of us until the whistle blew
and he was a crouched old man on a hospital inner tube

My father's bones shattered like glass and he died
worse than a dog so I forgave him

remembering his shy laugh glints of gold
in his long old teeth

Two funny stories maybe three and no one knew him
His skull in death an old Ojibwa's
*   *   *   *
At night the familiar hocus pocus of moon and mind
You soft in shadow that other
I know myself by

Come Light warm me
Sit on my grandmother's shoulder
who reads me through measles and chickenpox
bringing the world and New Orleans
in two blue suitcases

Light on the banana tree tallest of grasses
Light in her hazel eyes
*   *   *   *
Salt sand of the desert the long unfolding white of it
Out there I stole my bride from the land of the untouchables
Spirit me away dawn of the cockcrow
Light of my wavering window
*   *   *   *
My one great photograph you naked on a chaise lounge
eight months pregnant sleeping in the sun
light circling your circles
and one long draped arm

Light of the moment and always
*   *   *   *
Our son came out a greased chicken when he was born
and shone in the light of all subsequent Christmases

He seemed too small to take home
I had to learn to hold his head up

Your breasts engorged made you the gaudy
fertility goddess carved on a wooden salad spoon
I remembered from childhood

I gave him his first bath
Danced him heart to heart
Happy on the high hill of our summer
*   *   *   *
And happily I am already dead in a book somewhere
but in the dark closed pages or the light of a window
I don't know

To think I was ever a blank page
a tabula rasa a salt flat
a star

Hold the light at the window I am coming
though my knees ache
*   *   *   *
I have always enjoyed near the Equator
how sun maps a face
though I live in the snow

I was young in the sun of tennis courts
Pure form and goat mind
fencing the air

before the flat-light green-haze of hospitals
moon men in surgeries
Mother a mirage in the midnight
arriving from Rome

Stars of Paris outside my window
The girl I held in the dark for 13 years
against my loneliness

swims in the sun of the Pacific now
or is dead
*   *   *   *
I made love on a red cliff over the Mediterranean
at midnight in the cove of Los Pinos
to a woman from another language
beautiful as a mermaid
and hairy as a 23-year-old
I was young dumb in a hurry
No star touched my soul
*   *   *   *
When I think of light I think of salt flats or snow
though its jewels in the leaves are delectable
and fire your black hair

All these summers I've watched you garden our gold hill
Your hillocks not bad Old Woman

raised like prayer

Names of flowers elude me unless I look them up
Is it the desert in me or a dark mind
that cannot name these belles of light

My first garden was elephant ears and banana trees
and blunt nosed tortoises I kissed on their blunt noses
mossy bricks of the patio
a slight breeze I still recall
on my heat-rashed two-year-old naked buttocks

At three and a ward of the Church
I wanted to bathe with the Deacon's
13-year-old daughter Mary Katherine
because I liked her pubic hair
how it swirled in the warm water

One or two baths and everyone thought better of it
From then on it was Morgan or Hank

And still my life seems strange
I think my lake the Danube sometimes
or remember the pale lime-thick turquoise of the Karoon River
an eel under my left foot
in a shock of wonder

Salt flats and snow and the gardens between
*   *   *   *
Wherever it was light wanted to go
I said Yo Dis here is America
Let's do-si-do
Dat old Walt Whitman he big he kind
but boring

Which tribe am I
The twang the drawl the Yankee clipper
Which thrum of weathers
Which codes and netherworlds
Which beestings on the tongue

Or is the eye my alibi
and crude syntax
*   *   *   *

The eye that travels
sees still waves from airplanes
thunderless beaches

In the border towns
of the dead and nearly dead
comes dawn's bleak windows

The casualties were
entirely justified
say the generals

And all that flat line clarity is light

But what of the gutturals of evening
the festooned flesh and ornamental slang
the topsy-turvy muscles of a million mutabilities
carnal carnivals and carnivores
boardwalk bazaar bodega
heartstrings of the tongue's thrumming

when light of the blood is a kind of light
*   *   *   *
I drummed through the booze jungles of Bangkok
at age 15 door to door whore to whore
till one just 17 took me home to meet the folks
and wash me in the kitchen sink
It was intimate chilling a grim mirror
and in the sickly light of the bare bulb
she was truly beautiful
How much of her may have wished to dance
on my grave I don't know
*   *   *   *
Angels and vaginas the angels are
vaginas says my sculptor friend in his studio
when I find his new seraphim
stock and static

Stepping back I see it
Yes
if thighs had wings surely we could fly

From a dark declivity a few curlings
broadening into fern fronds
and baroque arabesques
a vertical mouth for a trunk
and the tree of life is any man's wife
*   *   *   *
And then there were the horses of the sun
ablaze over the clattering rooftops of the world
or at least Khuzistan with its rock hills
and smugglers' trails
A heartbeat between the knees
A breathing like the very wind
Flying the flags of themselves in their girlish manes
the foolishness of all our fathers in their wild eyes

In a monoprint I bought from a friend
three horses graze in a pasture
that might be cloud
the passionless horses of dream or a far field
closer to me now than the horses of wind and fire
muscle and bone
though I miss their salt scent
the rivers of sweat mapping the veins of their necks

Or maybe my friend's print is a dream of horses
dreaming their pastures dreaming their clouds
dreaming the artist dreaming of horses
whose absence is light
around the dark remembered bodies
*   *   *   *
When my horse the fastest in all Khuzistan died
I was away at college and knew in an instant
my childhood had ended
I tried writing a poem
but couldn't get the Braille of his skin
under my fingers onto the page
He'd lent me the great thunder of his body

and I had lain on his flanks in his stall while he slept
We loved each other with humor like brothers
On the day of our triumph he had blown by
Star of Persia to win by 20 lengths
He nickered and snorted when he heard my footsteps
and when I did not come for months he died
His life blessed mine as only animals can bless
Sometimes our betrayals are mindless as wind
and a man moves emptier than the child that had been
*   *   *   *

Moon of my mind with your long black hair
Come nearer sit opposite
Let me paint you the girl in the rattan chair
one full breast exposed
one knee drawn up that hides the other
A portrait in shadow but the light of the room

Or now the wise handsome woman Penelope old
whom Odysseus fears taking his eyes off
in his fog of years
The firm cool cheek and coolish eyes
and fires that flicker at night
along her spine

Flesh is not sexy to an old man's eye
until defied by gravity the slightly
slipped buttocks that affirms some pride
the waist loosening its stays
that still has grace
the back that arches that's known some ache
Of course it helps he knew the girl
entwined back in that Ithacan Eden world
neither of them doin nothin
that wouldn't make her mama's hair curl
*   *   *   *

The song of the desert is the song of oases
the white sand and midnight blue
of Persian Miniatures

In college I took the Luscher Color Test
"not a party game" we played

as a party game

The colors you chose showed your balance of mind
the book said and I got four asterisks
which meant not even with psychological counseling
would my mind be right

I saw the cultural bias of course
bright yellow and cool green
being the colors of Switzerland on a nice day

I chose burnt orange and a warm brown
the colors "only refugees" had chosen
the colors of Iranian cliff towns

Third I chose a dark blue
which meant according to the book
I used sex to block my fears
of various underworlds and my sense of doom

O well
The pipes of Pan play
as the pipes of Pan do

And it was a midnight blue
the color of oases
the cry of loons
*   *   *   *
In a glaze of light
the desert men of the high plateau
have faces like worn shoes
Descendants of Alexander's men
their gazes impassive over wide valleys
their stories as cadenced
as Omar Khayyam

Goats jangling like temple bells
they take tea in a circle
talk with their hands
haggling the prices of horses

I know nothing of their wives
or daughters
shadowy sometimes giggly in the doorways
*   *   *   *
No massing of light on a sundown cliff face
was ever more magical than the changing light
in our son's face

The garden gnome crouching at your side
primed to know name and each thrilling step
of each new planting his voice
of query and awe a small
very silvery bell

His little collie Tommy carved trails
into our deep thickets and taught him the woods
quail raccoon an occasional fox
a big black stray he glowered down
like the wrath of God
He died on one of those trails on a sunny day
at just age 10 with a single yelp
Our son's wail like a knife in the heart
lasted forever

What could I teach him the world
is sometimes like a poem but mostly isn't
Distrust money men corporate slogans pompous diction

The larger he grew the smaller I seemed

Now he has sideburns like Jim Bowie
and slouches in the sun where he walks

We hope he'll learn to think
*   *   *   *
I wanted to write a poem
whose first line anticipated its last
a box of inevitability
an inevitable box

But life is not like that
Life is a Bob Dylan song
that might go anywhere
or become mumbly and indecipherable

Tramps train whistles a bad sky

We wait for the refrain
Buzzards are circling the bad sky
Tramps enter the train whistles
and then the far blue mountains

But we have faith
Beauty is also circling we think
We wait for the refrain
*   *   *   *
And there you are again in the garden
after long winter and long years
your sports car body our chiropractor
complains you treat like a truck
your mud wife duds a swatch of black earth
glazing your forehead
radiant
pensive
dreaming garden again out of the squalor
of sticks and mud the sprawled
scrawled skeletons
There's no light I'd rather enter
than this sun on our porch in late March
the bare trees on the far hills rusting with inner fires
the lake ice jagged and scarred
and about to vanish

And we could vanish too Love
become wolves on our ancient hill
our tails still plumed and playful
our eyes still fires

a little blood on the sumac leaves
their wands waving toward a new autumn

Book X:

THE DARK MOTHERS

This day departs. It was a seed
of cold light that returned to its pod,
to its dark mother, to be reborn.

—Pablo Neruda, *Still Another Day*, XXV
translated by William O'Daly

Ancient Music

All-ee All-ee In Come Free
All-ee All-ee Outs In Free
Ollie Ollie Oxen Free

Ourselves our secrets released from hairy shadows Mother trees
we came bewitched by stars and insect scratchings
We were ghosts made of black mist
We were silent as stones
We had no faces
loud hearts
We felt steely and cruel
like Greeks on a night raid
We came floating like fireflies
toward a language only half our own
Our fathers smelled like Scotch
our mothers like strange flowers
We came lightly padding on our dark animal souls
who knew vanishing was an art
and returning was easy

All-ee All-ee in come free
All-ee All-ee outs in free
Ollie Ollie oxen free

Mary (1901-1991)

In that city of black iron lace and Gullah talk,
sin sashaying in shadow, I see you walk
down Pirate's Alley, the quick click of your heels
too Episcopal for the tolling of St. Louis's twelve-tongued bells—
a tea rose in a carnival of azaleas—
white-gloved, sky blue, crisp as your forbearers of Sloane Square
yet frankly forgiven in the not quite sultry air
of Easter, taken in by the wide river-mouth patois
of slithering shadows on darkened stairs
in just glimpsed courtyards

and swallowed whole in the black rivers of music,
sirening souls, palaces of jazz-joy, the air thick
with spangled night. A slur of voices
and footfalls on the wet-black streets poised
in mid-summer. Bourbon, Decatur, great
boozy names rolled deep in the throat—
a swill of voices
like the night's breeze, tropical, luscious.
And yours in the plush garden of wrought-iron chairs
crackling like a voice on the wireless—
matter-of-fact as a boot sole,
yet fluttering, fluting its thrill
of the just-so.

You were my first mother in that city of flowering nights
and sweating patios. Duplicitous, cunning,
sometimes mad as a hatter,
you undermined your own daughter
to hold me in the tight
niche of your charms — there where Lafitte
strode and Napoleon's death mask
stared ceilingward, I see you flash—
old outlaw in a city of outlaws,
sainted in a city of saints,
"queers," "reprobates." You gave me awe
and madness, a taste for all things stained

and fallen.
You were my New Orleans,
your chasteness the flipside of the stripper's martyred gaze,
the sagging wistful gays
your courtiers, the wisteria your bloom.
Mary, they called you. Mary of the crossword puzzle and
                                        afternoon
tea, Mary of the rocks, Mary of situations,
whose fall from grace — divorced, shunned,
a bastard grandson and a strident, quick-tongued daughter—
was resurrection in a place of flowers

and music, of terraced talk
on the floating hills of passing nights.
I learned to walk,
your hand in my hand, your electric
voice in my ear.
Even over years, your letters came with the same click
and stutter, your "Angel" signature the relic
of some old family joke
I never quite got.

"The Velvet Bulldozer,"
your doctors whispered near your death.
Your shingles punished you for years,
your retinas detached, your hearing failed.
Only your mind kept ticking in its queer act of will.
In the end, you were vituperative and genteel
as any southern belle. Nurses scuttled.
Doctors deferred. But even their regard
could not hold you forever.
You died with a small sigh—

white in a whited field.

Alex (1929-2001)

1

No act of will or Psychic Hotline cant
can raise you from the "utility urn"
I bought you in from Jern's Crematorium
last week. You're done, Mom, and you shan't
correct my English, nor nothing rail nor rant
against forever more. No high dudgeon
antics can stir the pot. Not even Nieman
Marcus on credit card can make you less than spent.
Farewell to the 12 Minton place settings
you never used, and to the Stickley bed
big as a Roman bath — to the nightshade
and St. John's Wort, masseuse, bed-wettings,
panic calls, blindness — all that pricey dread—
and those who promised love that never came.

2

You were of course the damaged princess, downed
at seven by the osteomyelitis
in your forehead — surgery, leeches,
one eyelid frozen, headaches that would pound
and pound until you saw yourself as drowned
and then redeemed in your own helplessness.
Great doctors mumbled over you like priests
until the divorce lawyers came and found
your miscarrying mother drug addicted,
your rich daddy a secret queer and crazy.
The baffled judge at last left you to choose.
You were just 10. Your breathing grew constricted
and the courtroom walls leaned in. You told me
how the strange tears splashed on your new red shoes.

3

And so you chose the mother you would hate
by 17, who stole your friends and lied
and put on airs, while the new poverty tied
you to yourself like a bad smell. Late
to work one morning in the Gulf Coast heat
after a six-mile walk, you were mortified
to find deodorant on your desk, tied
up with a little ribbon of pure hate.
That was the day, perhaps, you swore off sweat.
Powdered, perfumed, your beauty cool as ice,
you wore a long red coat, stiletto heels.
When, like soft wind, you tucked me in at night
and whisked away into a world of eyes
and mouths and random men, I felt your steel.

4

I hear your sniff of violated privacy
as my man's hands riffle the soft innards
of your long bureaus — folded, layered,
immaculate, lush femininity,
but not quite lacy — wombs of secrecy
that hold old letters in frayed ribbons, half-heard
snatches of conversation like the words
of little girls whose coy hypocrisy
you loathed. Was it your father's shortness made
you crave tall men, with timber in their voices,
who glowered down at me like men on stilts?
Was it just irony the man you married
stood only five foot six and favored boys.
Still I hear the venom of your hissing silks.

5

"Jarvis, Elizabeth Alice," your great
grandmother, slips from a bottom drawer,
faded but lovely as a long-pressed flower,
at perhaps 17. I contemplate
her unstrung collar. She was maybe late
to come in for the photo session hour,
her hair windblown, a breathless now or
never slight parting of the lips. Her fate
was to become an itinerant schoolmarm,
revered for high intelligence and wit,
who married a young minister and raised
three daughters of a certain bearing, charm,
humor and piety. What doesn't quite fit
the story, though, are her eyes — wild, slightly crazed.

6

What tamed that wild gaze that did not tame yours—
the cold Michigan farm? —anxieties
by candlelight? —the sleepless ministries
to endless household needs? From bottom drawers
they all come tumbling out, the ancestor
church ladies. Your grandmother's diaries,
chock full of weather's cheery godliness,
tell nothing of herself, only her prayers
to better serve. They warmed the glittering ice
of those heartbreaking farms that made you cringe,
if family jottings be believed. White haired,
bleak boned daughters of the mad-eyed Alice,
they show up faded at the faded edges
of family picnics — wistful, shyly proud.

7

Your existential loathing of the family
tree came early. One minister seduced
proved quite enough. Even old "Elder" Brews-
ter of the Mayflower hung there in the leafy
branches your mother grew like Blake's Poison Tree.
Its roots were Charlemagne and Robert Bruce,
the Black Douglas and John of Gaunt. No half-truth
was squandered in her quest for ancestry
of might and merit. You were the poor daughter
who'd never measure up to that high-flown bunk
and didn't try. You sang your own mantra.
You were no Mary Ann, let alone "Junior."
You were no pious chip off the old stump.
You changed your name to Alexandra.

8

Not the carpool mother who sang I Like
Ike songs. Not the girl damaged by her father
who could not say no but not quite yes either.
Not she who made little me one May night
with a blond Mick prize-fighter without quite
conceiving what went on in the weeds there.
Not the petulant, angry daughter,
or even the bad mother or bad wife.
You wanted to exist uncategorically.
You wanted to be an original
created in the diamond moment. Not
for you the pain of being only
one woman. You desired to be impossible,
and stirred and stirred and stirred and stirred the pot.

9

You loathed your mother's wheeler-dealer lies.
She worried you could *be* but could not do—
and always two stories of what was true—
yours and hers, hers and yours in perfect symmetry—
her outward quest, your inward journey,
clashing like cymbals. Both your winds could woo
me. I just saw varying shades of blue—
you darker and she lighter, but the same sea.
You both loved words, and words kept you apart.
In the same room, I'd feel your grinding wills
like creaking oarlocks, both a little crazy
and both killed off by the same bad heart.
You read Proust. She read me Wordsworth's "Daffodils."
In different climes, you each got called "a lady."

10

You toyed with me with threats of suicide
that year I turned 11. Even then
I thought you were just putting me on
at least half the time. But of course I cried
and rubbed your back, and in my own way tried
to wrestle down your darkest demons
as if you were my double. And just once
I feared you'd kill me in my sleep — some tired
hotel in Switzerland as I recall.
We'd fought. You had been drinking pretty hard.
But I remember mostly how the lake
was blue as lapis and we were immortal.
The incident left us drifting apart.
We just let it alone for beauty's sake.

11

All family wars play out best with three.
"What can we do with Alex, what's anyone
to do with Alex," Grandmother would intone
when I was fourteen and thought life easy.
We'd settle in for a long night's breezy
confession of your sins. Crazy as a loon
sometimes, she had the storyteller's one
virtue — to forge some actuality
just as she forged diplomas that got her work.
You were the poor poet of introverted
glances, who saw not things but in their ideas
that fluttered mothily toward the Absurd.
For you communion lurked behind the words.
After dissecting you, we'd have our *brioche*.

12

You showed no great interest in your grandson
and hated any grandmotherly role.
The very appellation seemed to appall
you, as if threatening your sense of fashion
and proper distance. No cuddly fat munchkin
hugger you. It was all about control
and self-possession and your ghastly will.
The touch you craved was near another ocean
under the calm fingers of your masseuse.
What you could buy you could put trust in—
even to that huge, somber library
whose books you never bothered to peruse.
You were just out there like the last Victorian
dying amidst some phantom tea party.

13

With enough money nothing need be real.
You blew through seven hundred thousand,
a grand a month for your group psychic plan
alone. The rest, just baubles of the *haute* genteel—
Cartier clocks, drawers full of identical
designer suits in three sizes, not one
worn — scarves and sweaters numberless as sand,
and so on. Mostly it was pretty dismal
being you those last years, ordering things
through UPS to have a moment's friend
when packages arrived. Your eyes were failing
and liver functions — clear rememberings
of things that had not ever happened.
The sirens in your blood-starved head were wailing.

14

When it was clear the money had run out,
quite willessly you fell upon your sword,
refusing Laesix that your doctor ordered
and losing him for that. For one coquette
moment you tried to call a quick about
face, change your mind. Nurses were guarded—
it was too late now for that. You looked bored
and drifted back to sleep. And that was that.
Your new friend-cosmetician held your hand.
Another startled as she entered your room
and one bright blue eye held her in its death-chill.
There was no code blue or shenanigans.
You'd become bride to yet another groom.
The angry child kicking in your head lay still.

15

Your portraits we brought home filled several boxes—
from Shirley Temple days to the young Hepburn,
your slightly cocked head and cocked eyebrow turn
the gaze inward, despite the outward glances
at the demanding camera. Long eyelashes
veil the quick bright eye. Something flickers and burns
and smolders out. A certain porcelain
veneer distracts us from your beauty's darkness.
What you held dearest was your inner kingdom.
In most all the portraits, that shows up.
None of them hold the look I cherish—
that devil-may-care, slightly-over-the-top,
what-the-hell grin. That wink. It all said come
dance, little broody boy, it's all there is.

Lamentations

Lament 1

I sat on the edge of my bed and I wailed and I wept
and I wanted to be empty as wind
and avoid all this old man dying shit
all this piecemeal dissolution humiliation
I wanted to rise like the Phoenix like the sun
and be new in the morning like the sun
I wanted to be 56 forever everything still
almost possible you like a mirage
just ahead within reach a rainbow's
shimmering I wanted to walk in
content in my fate to be walking still walking
the ache in my knees both telling and reassuring
and you in the paper tiara from the party
Queen May aswirl in the ribbons of mock death
and resurrection and I knew making love
 to you would make me whole through the universe
and everything else the denouement the terrible denouement
weeping and keening holding the rags the bitter rags
and then I was empty as wind and quiet

Lament 2

I went to the place of the poem but it was small
and dark and smelled like the ancient dens of foxes
Time kept coming back to scratch at the door
Old words littered the walls as if to keep the damp out
Someone had lit a fire but the ashes were cold
and the spiders were everywhere
And there was such sadness in the spaces between words
so much nothingness in the everything they said
Why fear the nothingness but we do
How fear the meaninglessness which we are
Here is my voice hang it on a tree
Here is my shoe which remembers me
And beautiful were your black diamonds
like the beauty of the sea at night
the points and spires and breezes of the night
where you passed and I followed and the words went out
and I vanished

Lament 3

I wanted to steal the last word from Death I suppose
and the silkiest of thefts are the poems of moonlight
poems of the sea and vast deserts their premonitions
And yet the Angel of Death is all kindness we're told
leading us out into moonlight through cracks in the clouds
had we known had we listened as the terrible talons
of pain and undoing let go
                              let us pray let us hope
the last ravening moments no end of consciousness
but a beginning
                    let us hope let us pray
though your buttocks domes against my limp gizmo
are all I need tonight to shore me home

Lament 4

How shall I say goodbye to myself poor
Charles Bon in his New Orleans and his emptiness
his decadence and charm and poisonous knowledge
who yet found you beyond all luckiness or fate
Goodbye to the heart hurt by its own betrayals
the mind full of inconsequence and error
a voice too full of itself
knickknacks and charms and the color blue
the silent cries of trees and the lake's sheen
and the numberless leaves haunting the numbered days
The man of the hour is the skeleton in the sombrero
who lies down in the curves of the voluptuous senorita
to a clatter of bedpans in the wings and the cackling of the damned
I sang you the songs of your fiery bones
and the soft opening flower of a dying kiss
Farewell to the grief of days and the holy smell of roses
your face knees voice like water
thighs like snow and eyes full of sky
Your laugh startled me so so so long ago
My will such as it is I give to clouds and to dreaming
my bones to the cathedrals of sand
to the pottery shards of lost places
my eyes to the vulture who resembles me
my wishes to wind and my loneliness
to thousand-year-old trees and the deserts of desire
I loved you in the simplest of ways my girl
and this is my poem which has no ending

Lament 5

I can imagine the loneliness of widows unraveling
unwelcoming days and old men in shut rooms
measuring their meds losing their minds dates names
If only vanishing were easy an old movie maybe
the corny deathbed speech the melodrama
each bedside mourner a cameo and case study
You see it in the eyes the soul speaking eye to eye
for the last time drinking the last horizon
And the faces strange and the rooms we wake in
with a start the floor moving and the windows dark
are no more ours than the clouds are or the voices of children
Is it the book misplaced that makes me weep
or tortured animals slaughtered children rape
by bayonet or any gone world's going
My grandmother kept a book 85 years pressing
a four-leaf clover given by a friend when they were five
Isn't that worth more than walking on the moon
but nothing stays still straight or in place
but the mute dignity of bones
bones without memory bones without song
So let us go under the hill and over the sky
and let us be bones together

The Dark Mothers

are wailing for their lost sons.
For them little has changed since Moses
but the weapons. A grief ago, the desert wind,
the on and on relentless drone

of once soft women in the murmuring grass,
now crones of the hard afternoon light—
lizard skin and hands become bird claws,
unforgiving eyes, like the mirrors of time,

keening out of the dark towns of my past
the dirges of the young undone
in their animal prime, the I-in-eye
vanishing in the caldrons of oblivion
where once Zarathustra dreamed.

+   +

I planted for the goddess some small conifers
now taller than our house and touching the stars,
one a great monster swaying in the moonlight
like the headdress of Shiva
swaddling a dozen birds, a million crawling things.

Together we dance on forgetfulness
and the clouds become elephants.
So this is old age, where the light splinters and the dream
ricochets, and the so-what bird laughs
like Rembrandt's last self-portraits.

(But the poet wants only to speak of sky and the ocean
of sand, to point to the setting sun
with a shrug of indifference.)

+   +

The weight of the dead is in the weightlessness
of the vanished who gave you dimension.
The 8th-grade teacher with a Boston accent
who says repeatedly don't call me ma'am,
the east Texas "mammy" with a face like Louis Armstrong

who carries in her sainted flabby arms
the first skewers of guilt and self-loathing,

and so on and so on with the vanishing weight of being,
the slow dissolution of knowing and caring—

the stone door, the widow's wail,
the click of the lid.

                 +   +

And so she brings fire to the ragged dark
in the flare of her hipbones,
swirl of her thighs. Tapering fingers
seamstress nimble, spidery smooth.

And now your absence glows
in the vaults of her belly, toss of her hair.
The slippery dark dances. But already
she is elsewhere, tomorrow
or yesterday, phantom of your best self
curling into smoke — dawn inventing the near hills,
the charred black of your face bones

wobbling back into morning.

Winter Light

Like a long-legged fly upon the stream
His mind moves upon silence.
    W. B. Yeats, "Long Legged Fly"

He was only the pale winter light
listening. He was old. The woman
had come, shimmering like a tree
reflected in water, and given him eyes.
Now she was fading back into forest
where he could not follow. She hated
his dreary naps, lies. Eternity yawned
into the wavering salt flats of his youth
that had meant distance and loneliness
and something he could not name,
yawned into the land of the dead
where all the old ghosts stood like statuary
with no need for names. His mind
the black edge of a crow's wing,
it had been a long winter, a white desert.

He was listening.
   * *

     Armies on the move again
and the rice bowls empty. Bodies in the mountains,
bulging in rivers. A small man, unhoused
in a small boat, trying to save his skin.
In the palace a little wine under the indifferent
beauty of sky, a little sex, a little death.
And the stink of it, rape and the mad dance
among fires.
    Li Po trudging the hills far from home.
   * *
As if the sky itself were sluicing down
into their slumberous bodies: blue horses
in an orange field ablaze in late sun,
a kind of paradise of the moment, out of time
and therefore holy. At the edge of the field
a shadow, the menace of time. Or is it

188

the face with many lines gazing from the window
into the fragrance of horses, the draped manes
and long faces of peace in the grass, skin
that rippling makes the whole body smile.
The woman had shown him this, in her broad hips
and liquid thighs, the chime of her laugh.
     *   *

He imagined the up-thrust cathedral's burden of stone
poised impossibly on a mathematical notion,
moonlight streaming down through the clerestory—
all that blood-soaked stone aching to be light,
or if not light, wings—
voices glancing off stone muffled in the tall air,
officious whisperers, assorted saints, She
off in a corner encaved in her forest of stone,
only the Mother of God now,
not of the trees and grass.
     *   *

The Oneidas tell their stories only in winter
so that the snakes who hide behind leaves
cannot hear them—the way poems are made
so the thugs lurking behind walls
with their electronic gadgetry
grow blank as river stones.
In dreams I return to the hill people's
fires and drum circles, speaking my poems
to the dark full of sparks and fireflies.
A woman lay down like a black river there
in the moonlight drunk with poets.
     *   *

He came on the rank river of swarming humanity
and beautiful ochres
to the gold temple with its leafy chimes
pearling the air like the voices of insect angels—
the pumpkin headed, pumpkin colored monks
anonymous as flowers—
a place of exact thoughtlessness
stirred by a single tremulous note
like the smile of the sky itself.
Overhead in the voluptuary trees,
the white fanged, long tailed gods and goblins

chuckling like monkeys—
in the time before time in the reign of the tiger.
                *   *

He dreamed these things as the wind blew and the cold deepened
and the shadows behind his face
became a gathering of crows arguing with evening—
each caw a vanishing soul, each coal-black eye
ironic and insolent. Praise be
to the nefarious crow—carrion eater,
squawker, complainer—
Praise be to our allotted cup of blood.

The Way Out
(How It Started: The Train Station)

I was leaving the comfortable nest and warren life
of the shadowy French Quarter
when the great clanking, screeching, spark-spitting
dragon locomotives
set me dancing as if on hot coals
behind my mother's wide familiar skirts
as I learned the beginning of displacement is fear
67 years ago
like yesterday

a residual bubble on the river of I
   +   +
The long dead haunt me
who were the beautiful women
of my half-orphaned childhood
gliding naked in the bathroom steam
like Olympians, my mother's rosy nipples,
my grandmother's dark areolas
in the paradise of innocence.
Now even their bones are powder,
their spirits only the mists of my brain
and vanishing.
   +   +
In the middle ground tortured mountains under the ache of sun.
Long bray of the donkey in the valley of yesterday.
Ululating mothers. Dark
laughter. And who are you in the foreground
trying to take stock like a man in fog
in his circle of lantern light. The 50-year story of a worsening
                                                                limp.

   +   +
To walk out into the sun and not come back
is the promise of the desert,
the dream of its wavering lakes.
I now know more dead than living says my rolodex,
numbers I'll never call again: dear detritus.

I'm looking for the whisper
that says this matters
among the battering bartering voices
seeking their moment of importance,
their 15 seconds of resonance,
the moments between this and that
when the doors to our souls stand open
and waiting.
    +   +

I've been reading young men long dead
to decipher my ambiguous handprints.
They are neither here nor there,
my brothers in solitude, and a few sisters
who help me float. It's their floating I'm after
and a few feathery hints. I'm now. I'm not.
On/off. The flickering neon of a flung down
grunge country strip-joint under enormous
star-studded sky. The gone-ness of it all.
The space. The closeness.
How small we are
and grand.
    +   +

Time fans out in too-rich technicolor again
the tulip fields of Holland in a dollhouse world
with tiny wooden bridges,
my motorcycle throbbing like a heart,
like a plundering dynamo,
like thunder.

I was a demi-demon riding the thunder
in a dollhouse world.
    +   +

The living echo summons the lost body like a voice in a dream.
Walking in a hiss of rain on a roadway
a recalcitrant ghost, the everyman slouch of resistance.
Through the trees a glistening lake,
an eye peering up from the underworld
amazed and amazing. We search for the rainbow.
We hunt for ourselves. We honor the sun.
    +   +

192

I believe in the God of Hafez, sky
becoming woman becoming sky again,
great stretch of the infinite scented with rosewater
or orange blossoms in a shady bower.
I have ridden that sunbeam
of summer gold and the moonbeams
of silent adoration, my body
now an old leather coat I must soon slip off
to enter the summoning river of absence.
  + +
And the sky is not empty but open
says the dead poet who stands in for us all
in this poem of slippery slopes
and kneeling grass,
glittery shards and non-sequiturs.

The sky is not empty but open.

Book XI:

LOST HALLWAYS

See the water

in my cupped hands
emptying itself of me.

—Malaika King Albrecht, "The Present Moment"

Around Sundown: The Wandering

I love you for this house you made and rearranged for 40 years,
paintings quickening the walls, migratory books in piles,
and outside, fringes of flowers and sprawling jungle grass—
all light as your light passes through

although tonight you claim that phantom house
with finer lines of vision— the art more deftly synced,
the view under stairs more shadow-striking—
and cleaner planes to hold the ceiling up,

the house you dream I cannot enter.
Mine is the one cluttered with old age detritus,
messy counters, clothes in heaps,
yours just newer, lighter,

though you must ask which door to use
and if it's dawn or night, whether we'll meet tomorrow
or next week, and if you'll need your purse.
I love you for the lamplit ghosts of songs

in poems shared and bodies flared and winged,
and say it's here, despite the clutter,
this house so like the one you dream,
but know it's lost to you at end of day,

this end of time slipping into ruin,
this garden-circled place fading into gloom.

Today You Become

the many headed Hydra
saying "you've never seen
where I live," now stalking
down our road in multi-tilt
dimensions. Will you be safe?
Will your anger at my obtuseness
keep you watchful for the sudden
sweep of fender around our bend?
High dudgeon has its amplitudes
and confessions, its focus and blindness,
kicking free the shackles of insult and guilt—

the world old as we are now
who made love to the beat of ancient stones
and walked our crooked miles
of crooked seasons
lovely in their vanishings.

Her Laugh

Can Suzy come out to play
the child in me wishes to say.
Can she dance in the field,
twirl her hair in the breeze,
maybe kick up her heels,
say love as you please

as grass does the light
or the lake takes the storm?
Can she flow through the night
all liquid with form?
Oh tell me O house on the hill,
can Suzy come out to play

though dusk's come in with a chill
and taken her laughter away?

Undertow

Where is it the clock ran?
How cold the ancient entryway!
You see me in two

like a knife knifing the eye.
How wise is a mirror?
You are too many ghosts to attend to

and make for the darkest of weathers.
I feel your many-ness.
I chase your dissolve.

Maybe after a deep dive
we will come up for air
and remember.

When We Danced

Light was the dance and the dance was light
O dizzying dish of my demise,
dervish of those long-ago faded Levi's—
I see us still,
stark, illuminated in the chill,
a chaliced stillness in the tottering night.

Lost Hallways

The music makes you smile and stills my soul.
The past drifts back, flotsam and jetsam
of a lost treasure ship, our heroine
going down to Davy Jones—her face,
less mobile but still beautiful
and darkly haunted now.
                                    I dread
the minutes like whipcracks, help you
into clothes and down lost hallways—
treat you like a toddler till you say
"I can't find my heart,
I'm just all tears and nothing else."

We Ban the News

as every wound
becomes your wound, all tears your tears.
With no capacity to distance, Ukraine
outside your window, your tribe's
the Poor, the Damaged and the Lost
among the skulls of broken cities—
a child's doll
half visible in the rubble.

Our Luck

runs out like sand through an hourglass—
your beauty once like the new-fallen snow
now shades to gray, the color of our winter's
long months to come.
                              I cannot hold you
or let you go. Still days darken.
Black trees bow in wind.
                              We've lost
our way in the worst of seasons
in the whorl of the guffawing crow,
our garden gone to seed, our eyes
like Homer's falling heroes'
going black.
                              I remain perhaps
your last plucked flower
in the wilt of my will.

Looking for the Door

You can no longer lie down without help
and my anxiety gut tightens
and churns. I'm looking for the door
in a room without doors, my grief
god-sized and implacable.
Who can I bargain with?
Once we were shuddering
interchangeables, silvery fish
in a pod of perfect
ballet.
      Now I move you about
like an armload of lumber,
your muscles stiff with uncertainty,
your face vaguely fearful.
I yearn to give birth to you, feel you
unfold like our floppy magnolia
blossoms in spring, lavish and lovely
in their lascivious come-ons.
I long for that fluency and fiery freedom
against this hardening ossification,
this deaf call to stillness.

Our Absence

stretches out, the long haul
of a short future, the unsaying
of lost conversations, love's erasures
and grievances, half-smiles, pain groans,
night sweats. I love you, I love you, I love you
but can no longer remember
the contour of it, the smoke of it, your fire
in the quickening twilight.
I hate you, I hate you, I hate you
sing the demons of my forgetfulness.
Cursed by my myriad blessings
and the silk of your skin
I ease you into sleep.

CODA:

THE LOOK BACK

Once
(with some thefts from Simon Behbehani)

I came to you as if from a far country
The night was not quite in your eyes
but the evening smoke and the roses of your skin
met in purple shadows

I came through the vague veiled streets
toward some clarity or hunger
You were my fire in the moth-light
my confessor

You danced the stars blind under the witching moon
I crawled in your darkness like the tapping beetle
Our mouths met

Dawn in the desert is a million gold butterflies
I lived there once among broken stones
husks of bodies
a tale of death and deaths
and women turned to salt
under stubborn hummocks of black cloth

We grow old like the cracking clay
of forgotten rivers
Soon no one will remember our voices
or the glancing light of our tremulous
tremors

Was it the wind I came on
lipping your waters
combing the sunlight scarves across your throat

So often now we are tired
and old women I once knew speak harshly
behind the curtain
and the mud of the riverbank
squelches under their feet

I came through bulrushes over moon-glazed bayous
and our bodies became snake-dancing
cranes
feathery cries

We cannot love each other forever
except as the stars do
all flame and nothingness

Our skins will grow worn and frail
as papyrus leaves
locust wings
May the burden of pain bring lightness

We lie down to take flight
like the desert sand under the scour of wind

I came like a sea eagle out of the sun's eye
to whirl you talon in talon
down the roller coaster sky

I met your gaze in the forest of being

The rest was just history

The Look Back

as the world slips away—
Sophia Loren in a floral dress
and barefoot, bombers overhead
in a story of walking.
This is the village where we began
more black and white than we had imagined,
some shaggy sheep on a hillside
and too little time.
We were there when the pillagers came
on their steaming horses
and someone was ringing a church bell.
We were there when the lovers
became entangled in death
in the indifferent grass
and we longed to open at the seams
and speak in tongues and fall to our knees,
the brown hills fading in the distance
and maybe an old man in an oxcart
inching toward the horizon
or our mothers weeping by the roadside.

ACKNOWLEDGMENTS

Poems included here previously appeared in the following:

Books:

When She Became You / Songs to Suzanne (Black Spruce Press) 2022
The Dark Mothers (Black Spruce Press) 2020
The Moon's Children (Kelsay Books, Aldrich Press) 2020
Where She Dances (FutureCycle Press) 2020
Summoning the Outlaws (Kelsay Books, Aldrich Press) 2017
Crossings: A Record of Travel, New and Selected Poems (Lamar University Literary Press) 2016
River Time (Wells College Chapbook Contest Winner, Wells College Press) 2014
Bone-Songs and Sanctuaries, New and Selected Poems (The Sheep Meadow Press) 2009
Once (Foothills Press) 2008
Silky Thefts (Orchises) 2007
Ghost Moon (Pine Press) 1997
Totems (Basfal Books) 1994
A Dance of Stone (Pine Press) 1984
Bone-Songs and Snctuaries (chapbook, Pine Press) 1984
The Hardman County Sequence (Heliographis) 1980

Anthologies:

Contemporary Surrealist and Magical Realist Poetry, an International Anthology edited by Jonas Zdanys (Lamar University Literary Press) 2023
Earth Care (anthology. Ed. Martin Willitts Jr., Willet Press) 2022
Lament 2, from *Lamentations, Writing for Life* (Anthology), Nervous Ghost Press, 2020
Like Light, 25 Years of Poetry and Prose from Bright Hill Poets and Writers, 2017
From the Finger Lakes: A Poetry Anthology, 2017
Corresponding Voices 10th Anniversary Special Edition, 2017
World Poetry Yearbook 2015 (Earth Culture Press, P.R.China)

Corresponding Voices (2002 Anthology, Point of Contact Productions)

Magazines and Literary Journals:

Beloit Poetry Journal
Birmingham Poetry Review
Bitterroot
Bottomfish
The Chattahoochee Review
The Comstock Review
Ekphrasis
Graham House Review
The G. W. Review
Kansas Quarterly
The Northern Review
REAL: Regarding Arts and Letters
The Sewanee Review
Song
The Southern Poetry Anthology, Volume VIII: Texas
The Southern Review
Stone Canoe
Tar River Poetry
Vanderbilt Review
Vitruvius (online)

Additionally,

"Old Mountains" was runner-up in the Rome Arts Center's Milton Dorfman International Poetry Contest in 2002; a small recorded selection won the 2017 Miller Audio Prize in Poetry sponsored by the Missouri Review and judged by Vijay Seshadri; the series of poems in the first section was completed under the auspices of a New York State Creative Artist Public Service Grant and first appeared with Dorothea Lange's photographs and Foreword by W. D. Snodgrass in the limited edition book *The Hardman County Sequence*; and a previous collection containing many of these poems, *Crossings: A Record of Travel,* was given the Best Poetry Book of the Year Award by the Downtown Writers Center of Central New York sponsored by the Gifford Foundation in 2016.

The poems in the section called "Where She Dances" owe much to the paintings and photographs of Darryl Hughto, and many of those in "Before Speech" to photographs by the late Scott Ian Barry.

My gratitude to all—with special thanks to Mark Raush for permission to use his painting, *Stone Wash*, as the cover image, and to Bruce Bennett for his invaluable editorial advice and years of support.